Terrific practice for White Rose Maths from CGP!

This super CGP workbook is matched to the White Rose Maths Scheme of Learning — great for helping pupils work on their skills.

It's jam-packed with questions for every block and small step of the Year 4 Autumn Term — so you know it has everything pupils need.

Plus there are plenty of Problem Solving and Reasoning questions to check they know their stuff. Oh, and don't forget, we've included the answers to every question online — just scan the QR code at the end of the contents page. You're welcome!

What CGP is all about

Our sole aim here at CGP is to produce the highest quality books — carefully written, immaculately presented and dangerously close to being funny.

Then we work our socks off to get them out to you — at the cheapest possible prices.

Contents

Block 1 — Place Value

Step 1 — Numbers to 1000 1
Step 2 — Partitioning to 1000 2
Step 3 — Number Lines to 1000 3
Step 4 — Thousands 4
Step 5 — Numbers to 10 000 6
Step 6 — Partitioning to 10 000 8
Step 7 — More Partitioning to 10 000 9
Step 8 — 1, 10, 100 and 1000 More or Less 10
Step 9 — Number Lines to 10 000 11
Step 10 — Estimating on Number Lines 12
Step 11 — Comparing Numbers to 10 000 14
Step 12 — Ordering Numbers to 10 000 16
Step 13 — Roman Numerals 18
Step 14 — Rounding to the Nearest 10 20
Step 15 — Rounding to the Nearest 100 21
Step 16 — Rounding to the Nearest 1000 22
Step 17 — Rounding to the Nearest 10, 100 or 1000 23

Block 2 — Addition and Subtraction

Step 1 — Mental Adding and Subtracting 24
Step 2 — Adding Numbers with No Exchanges 25
Step 3 — Adding Numbers with One Exchange 27
Step 4 — Adding Numbers with More Exchanges 28
Step 5 — Subtracting Numbers with No Exchanges 29
Step 6 — Subtracting Numbers with One Exchange 31
Step 7 — Subtracting Numbers with More Exchanges 32
Step 8 — Subtracting Efficiently 33
Step 9 — Estimating Answers 34
Step 10 — Strategies for Checking Answers 35

Block 3 — Area

Step 1 — Area 37
Step 2 — Counting Squares 38
Step 3 — Making Shapes 40
Step 4 — Comparing Area 42

Block 4 — Multiplication and Division A

Step 1 — Multiples of 3 43
Step 2 — Multiplying and Dividing by 6 44
Step 3 — 6 Times Table Facts 46
Step 4 — Multiplying and Dividing by 9 47
Step 5 — 9 Times Table Facts 49
Step 6 — 3, 6 and 9 Times Tables 50
Step 7 — Multiplying and Dividing by 7 51
Step 8 — 7 Times Table Facts 53
Step 9 — 11 Times Table Facts 54
Step 10 — 12 Times Table Facts 56
Step 11 — Multiplying a Number by 1 and 0 58
Step 12 — Dividing a Number by 1 and Itself 59
Step 13 — Multiplying 3 Numbers 60

The **answers** to every question in the book are available **online** — to find them, scan the QR code on the left or go to cgpbooks.co.uk/rose

Published by CGP

Editors:
Molly Barker, Liam Dyer, Sammy El-Bahrawy, Alison Palin,
Caley Simpson, Julie Wakeling, Hannah Wilkie

"White Rose Maths" is a registered trade mark of White Rose Education Ltd.
Please note that CGP is not associated with White Rose Maths or White Rose Education in any way.
This book does not include any official questions and is not endorsed by White Rose Education.

ISBN: 978 1 83774 176 2

With thanks to Joanne Robinson and George Wright for the proofreading.
With thanks to Jade Sim for the copyright research.

Clipart from Corel®

Printed by Elanders Ltd, Newcastle upon Tyne.
Based on the classic CGP style created by Richard Parsons.

Text, design, layout and original illustrations © Coordination Group Publications Ltd. (CGP) 2024
All rights reserved.

Photocopying this book is not permitted, even if you have a CLA licence.
Extra copies are available from CGP with next day delivery • 0800 1712 712 • www.cgpbooks.co.uk

About This Book

- This book matches the White Rose Maths Scheme of Learning for Year 4 Autumn Term.
- It's split up into blocks, with each small step covered on one or two pages.

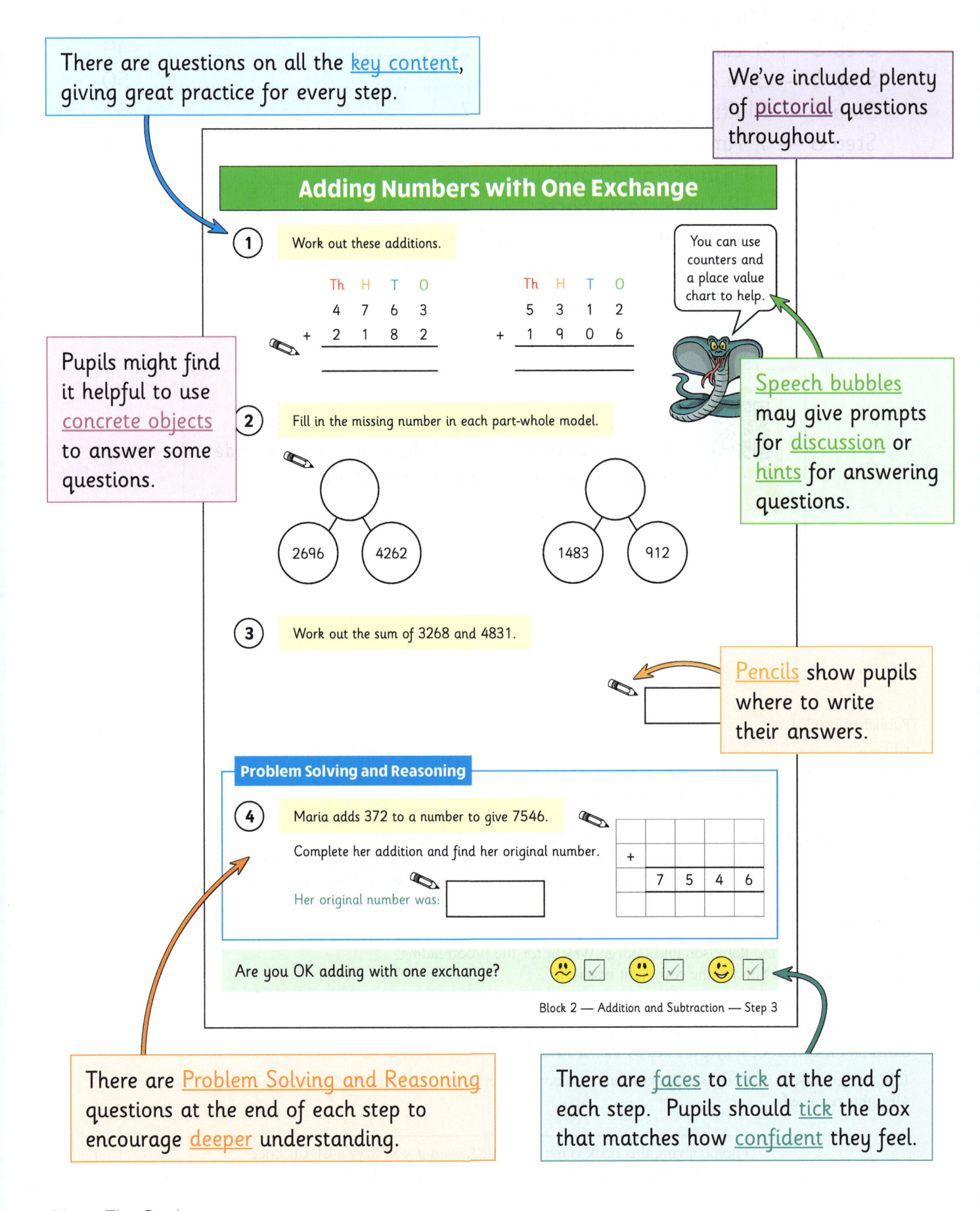

There are questions on all the key content, giving great practice for every step.

We've included plenty of pictorial questions throughout.

Adding Numbers with One Exchange

① Work out these additions.

Th	H	T	O
	4	7	6	3
+		2	1	8	2

Th	H	T	O
	5	3	1	2
+		1	9	0	6

You can use counters and a place value chart to help.

Pupils might find it helpful to use concrete objects to answer some questions.

② Fill in the missing number in each part-whole model.

2696   4262

1483   912

Speech bubbles may give prompts for discussion or hints for answering questions.

③ Work out the sum of 3268 and 4831.

Pencils show pupils where to write their answers.

Problem Solving and Reasoning

④ Maria adds 372 to a number to give 7546.

Complete her addition and find her original number.

Her original number was:

+				
	7	5	4	6

Are you OK adding with one exchange?

Block 2 — Addition and Subtraction — Step 3

There are Problem Solving and Reasoning questions at the end of each step to encourage deeper understanding.

There are faces to tick at the end of each step. Pupils should tick the box that matches how confident they feel.

About This Book

Block 1 — Place Value

Numbers to 1000

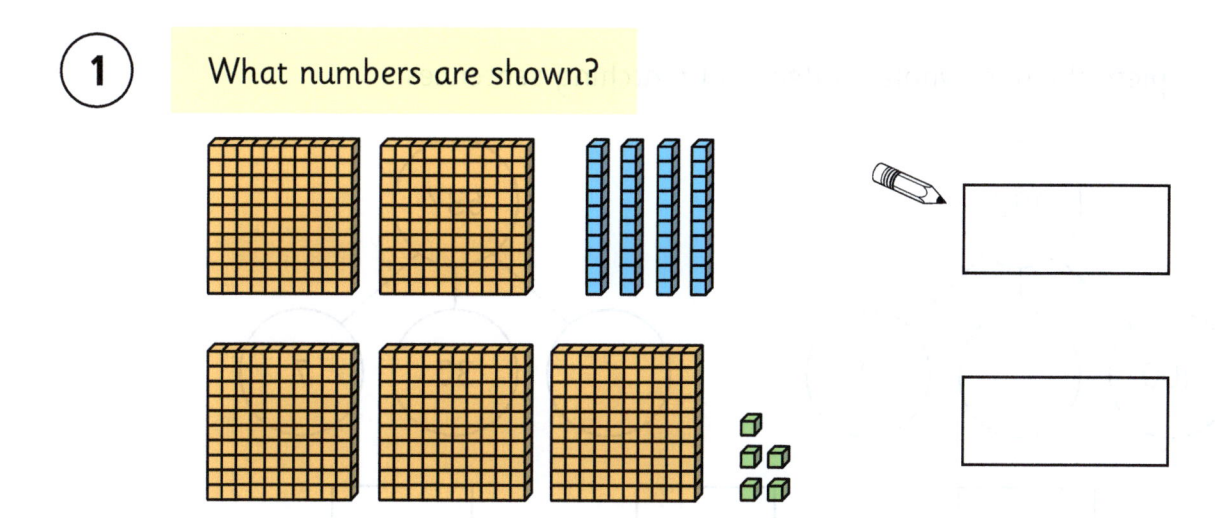

1 What numbers are shown?

2 Draw place value counters in the charts to represent each number. The first one has been started for you.

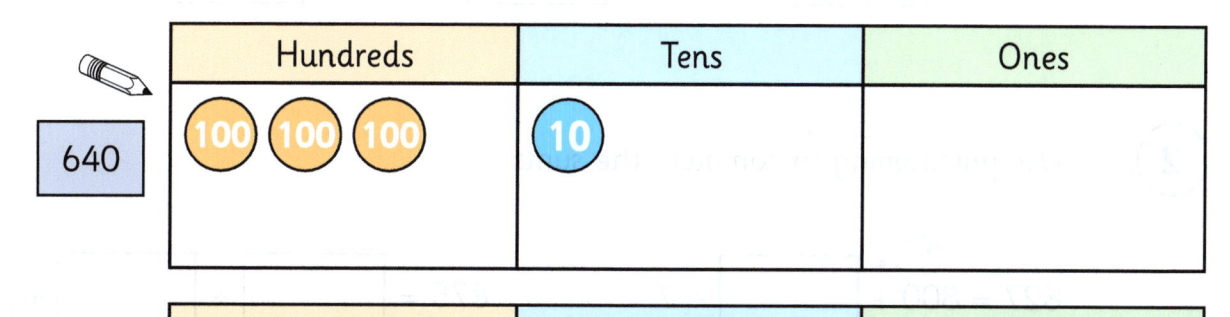

Hundreds	Tens	Ones
100 100 100	10	

640

Hundreds	Tens	Ones

406

Problem Solving and Reasoning

3 Boris has made a number using place value counters.

The number is three hundred and ten.

Explain the mistake that Boris has made.

What number do the counters represent?

How did you do?

Block 1 — Place Value — Step 1

Partitioning to 1000

1 Complete the part-whole models and matching sentences.

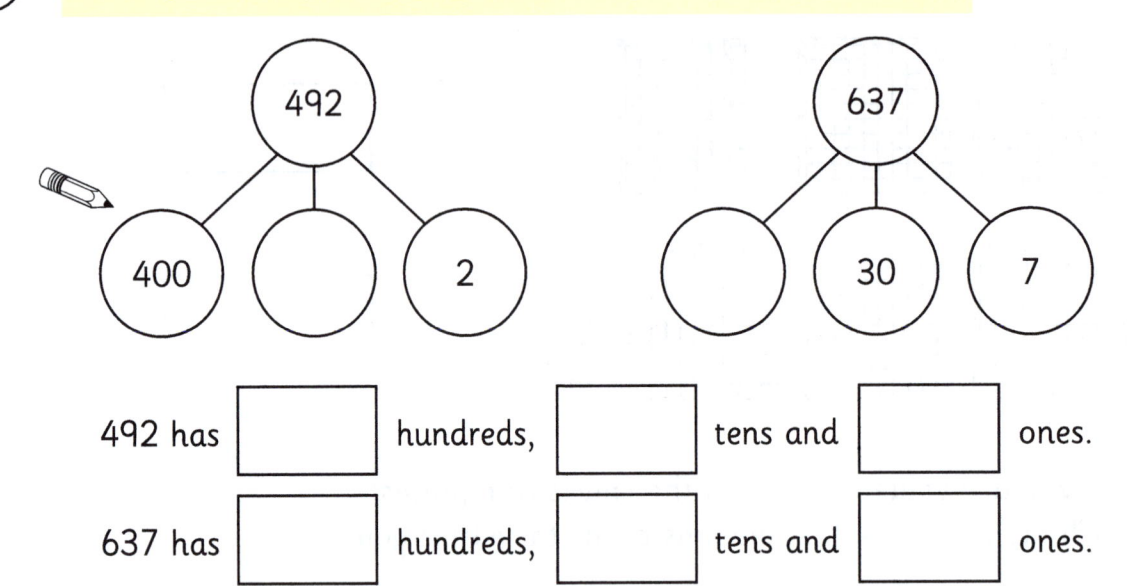

492 → 400, ☐, 2

637 → ☐, 30, 7

492 has ☐ hundreds, ☐ tens and ☐ ones.

637 has ☐ hundreds, ☐ tens and ☐ ones.

2 Use partitioning to complete the sums.

827 = 800 + ☐ + 7   875 = ☐ + ☐ + ☐

870 = ☐ + ☐   807 = ☐ + ☐

Problem Solving and Reasoning

3 Shanti has the four number cards shown. 8 2 9 6

She writes in her book:

> The largest 3-digit number I can make has six tens and two ones.

Do you agree with Shanti? Explain why.

Did you get all of that or just part of it?

Block 1 — Place Value — Step 2

Number Lines to 1000

1) What numbers are the arrows pointing to?

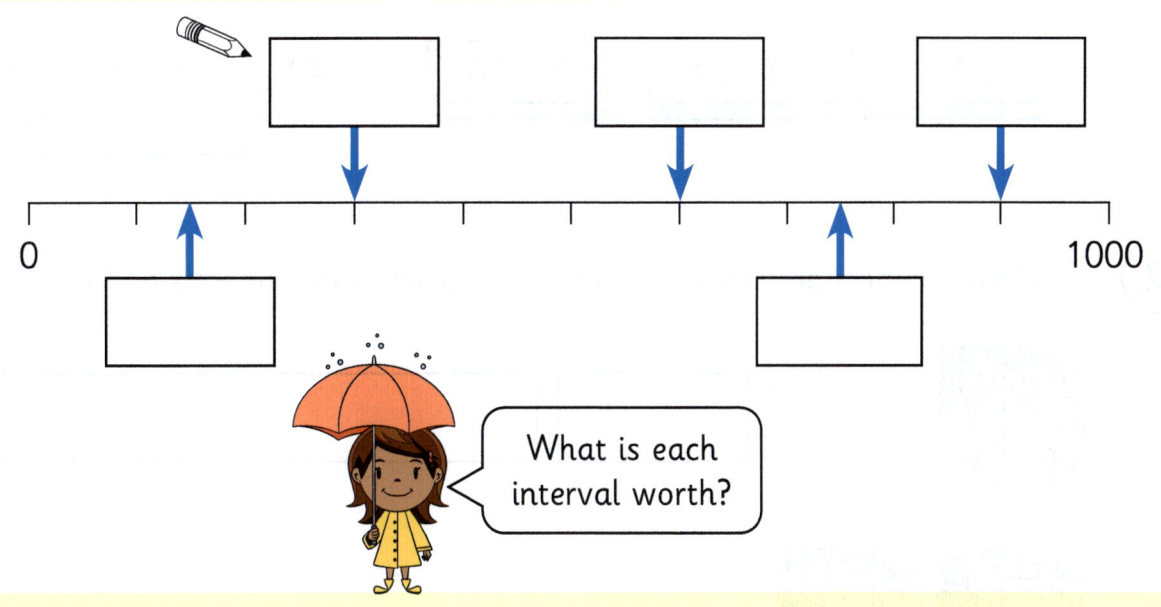

0 — 1000

What is each interval worth?

2) Draw arrows on the number line to show the positions of 600, 850 and 925.

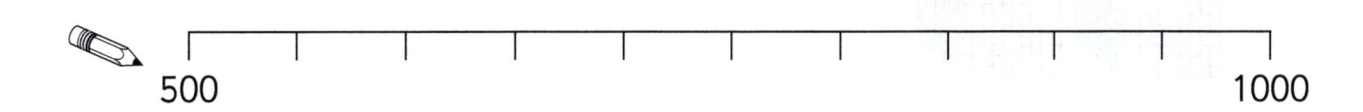

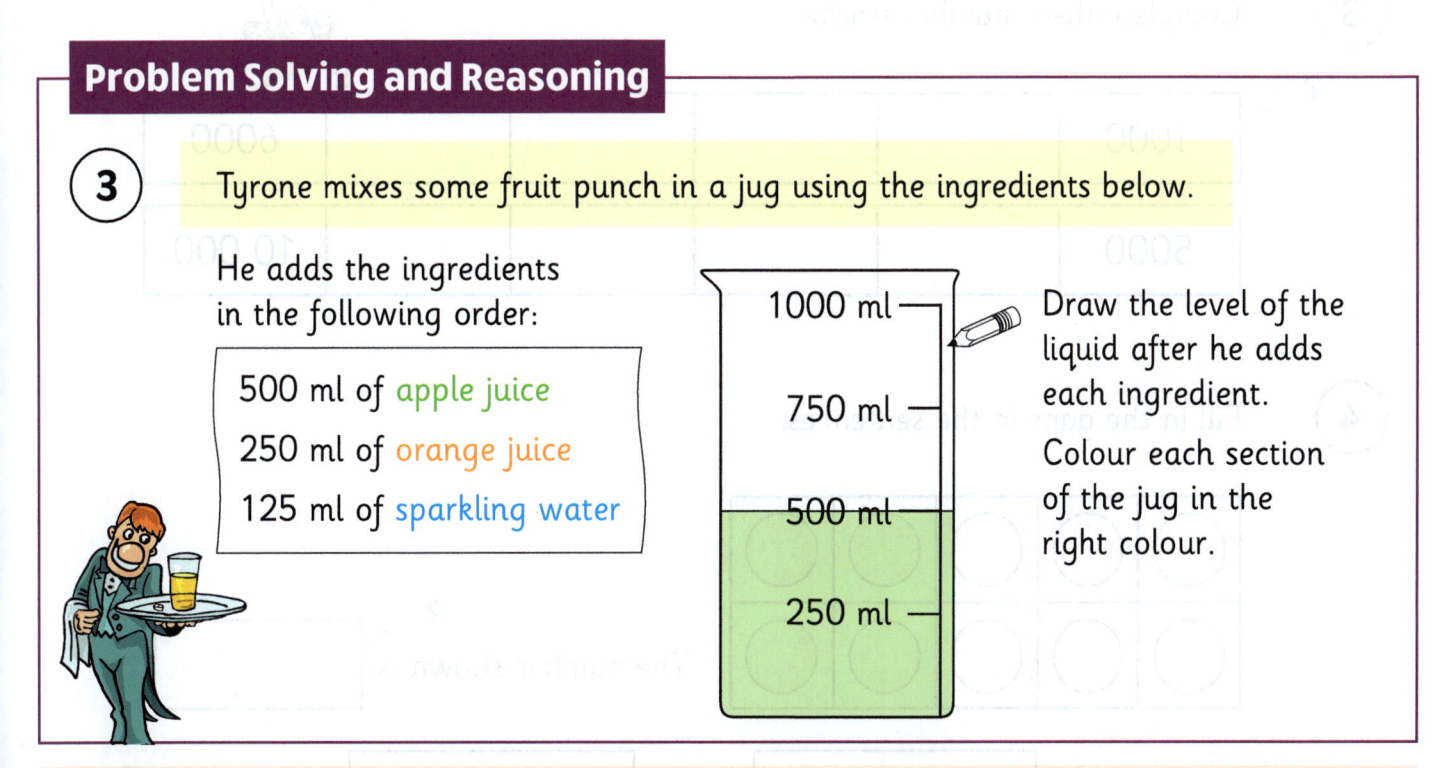

500 — 1000

Problem Solving and Reasoning

3) Tyrone mixes some fruit punch in a jug using the ingredients below.

He adds the ingredients in the following order:

- 500 ml of apple juice
- 250 ml of orange juice
- 125 ml of sparkling water

Draw the level of the liquid after he adds each ingredient.

Colour each section of the jug in the right colour.

Is everything lining up nicely for you?

Block 1 — Place Value — Step 3

4

Thousands

1 How many pieces are there altogether in these three jigsaw puzzles?

[1000] [1000] [1000] ☐ pieces

2 What numbers are shown? Write your answers in numerals and in words.

(1 thousand-cube) ☐ ☐

(4 thousand-cubes) ☐ ☐

3 Complete these number tracks.

| 1000 | | | | | 6000 |

| 5000 | | | | | 10 000 |

4 Fill in the gaps in the sentences.

(ten 100 counters)

The number shown is ☐ .

There are ten ☐ in one ☐ .

Block 1 — Place Value — Step 4

5 Fill in the gaps in the sentences.

2 thousands are equal to ☐ hundreds.

4 thousands are equal to ☐ hundreds.

30 hundreds are equal to ☐ thousands.

70 hundreds are equal to ☐ thousands.

Problem Solving and Reasoning

6 Poppy is thinking of a number.

I will start from my number...

...then count forward in 1000s until I reach 10 000.

If Poppy counts forwards 6 times, what is her starting number?

☐

7 Pete has used place value counters to show a number.

1000 1000 1000

My number is equal to 300 hundreds.

Is Pete right? Explain your answer.

Are you happy with your thousands?

Block 1 — Place Value — Step 4

Numbers to 10 000

1 Fill in the missing numbers.

There are ☐ thousands, ☐ hundreds, ☐ tens and ☐ ones.

The number shown is ☐ .

2 What numbers are shown?

What is the same and what is different about these numbers?

Block 1 — Place Value — Step 5

3 Draw counters to complete the place value charts.

4051

Th	H	T	O
●● ●●			

6080

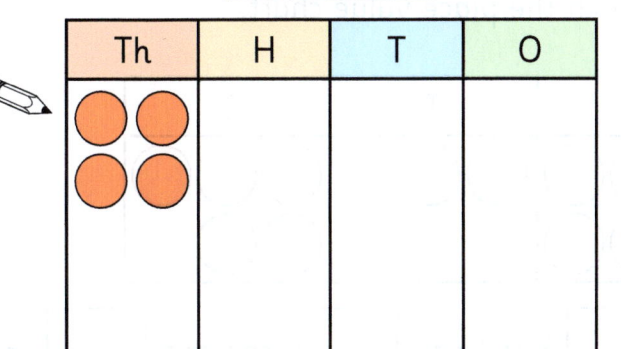

Th	H	T	O

4 Show the number 9532 on this Gattegno chart.

1000	2000	3000	4000	5000	6000	7000	8000	(9000)
100	200	300	400	500	600	700	800	900
10	20	30	40	50	60	70	80	90
1	2	3	4	5	6	7	8	9

Problem Solving and Reasoning

5 Maya is representing a number on a place value chart.

She has one counter left to place. ●

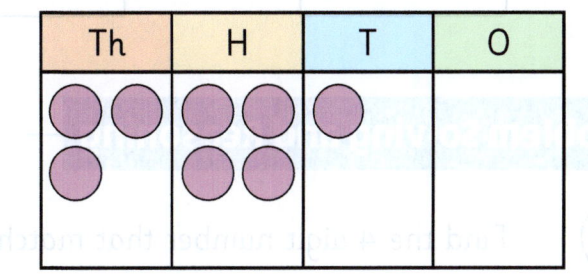

Th	H	T	O
●● ●●	●●● ●●	●	

Write down all the possible values of her number.

Have you shown those numbers who's boss?

Block 1 — Place Value — Step 5

Partitioning to 10 000

1 Fill in the missing numbers to match the place value chart.

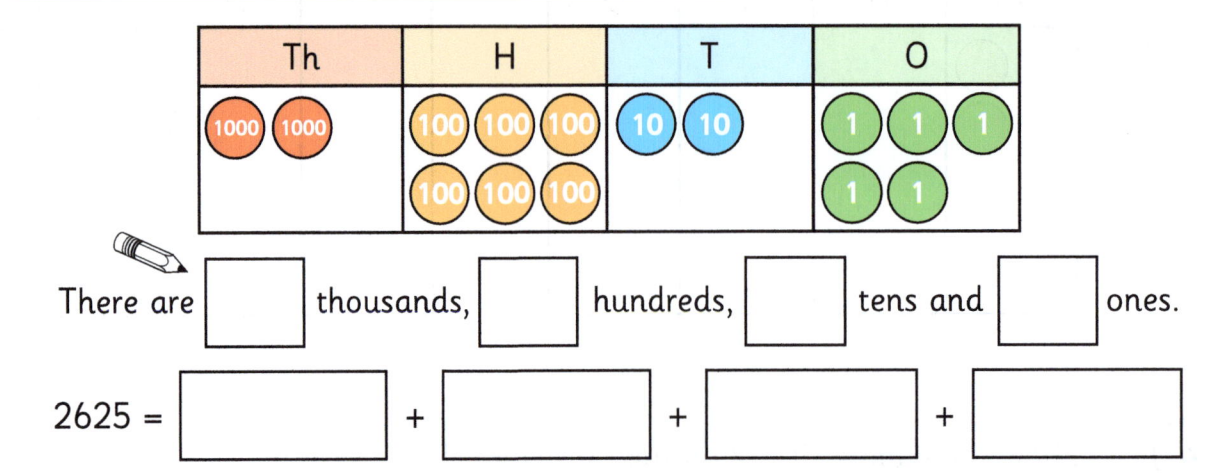

Th	H	T	O
1000 1000	100 100 100 100 100 100	10 10	1 1 1 1 1

There are ☐ thousands, ☐ hundreds, ☐ tens and ☐ ones.

2625 = ☐ + ☐ + ☐ + ☐

2 Complete the part-whole models and matching sums.

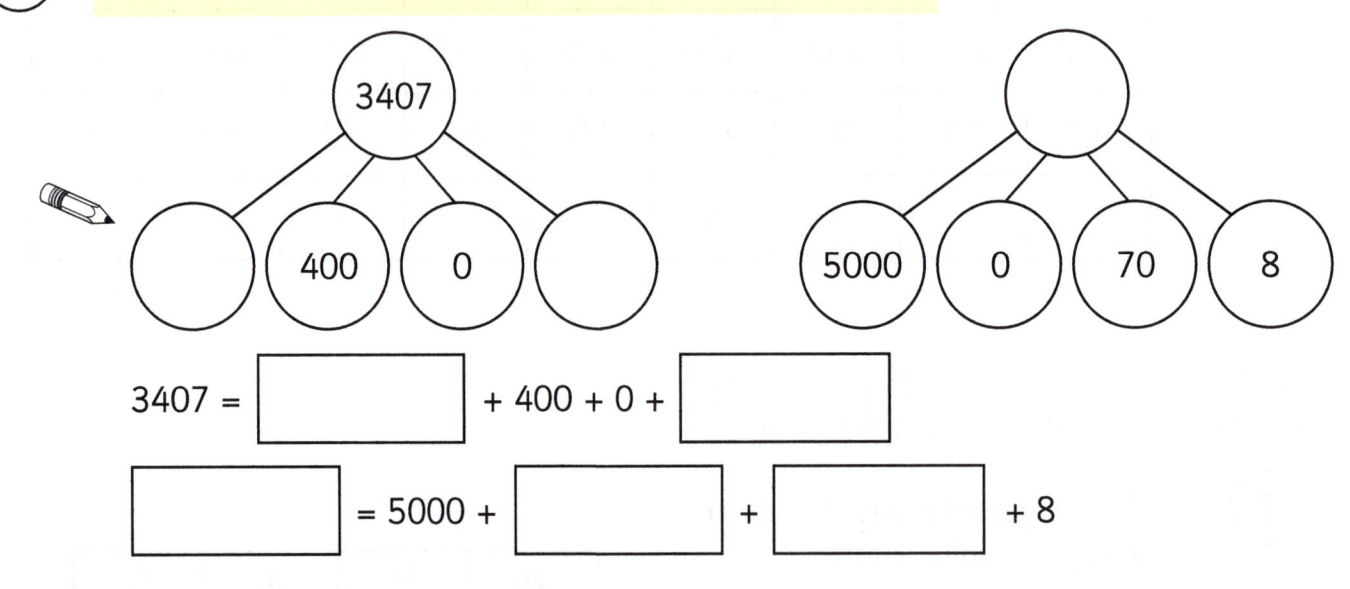

3407 → ☐, 400, 0, ☐

☐ → 5000, 0, 70, 8

3407 = ☐ + 400 + 0 + ☐

☐ = 5000 + ☐ + ☐ + 8

Problem Solving and Reasoning

3 Find the 4-digit number that matches these clues.

- The digits add up to 10.
- The number is odd.
- The number has 3 hundreds.
- The thousands digit is two more than the ones digit.

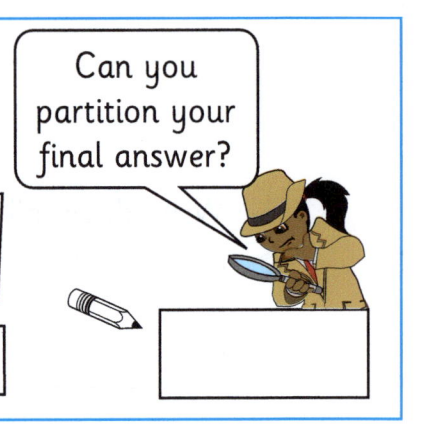

Can you partition your final answer?

Have you got this figured out?

Block 1 — Place Value — Step 6

More Partitioning to 10 000

1) Use partitioning to complete the sums.

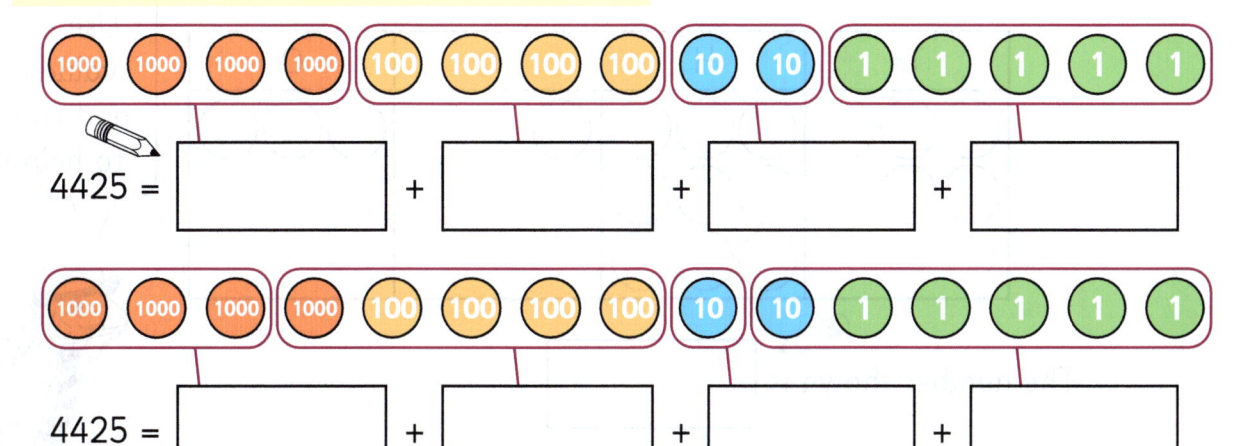

4425 = ☐ + ☐ + ☐ + ☐

4425 = ☐ + ☐ + ☐ + ☐

2) Complete the part-whole models.

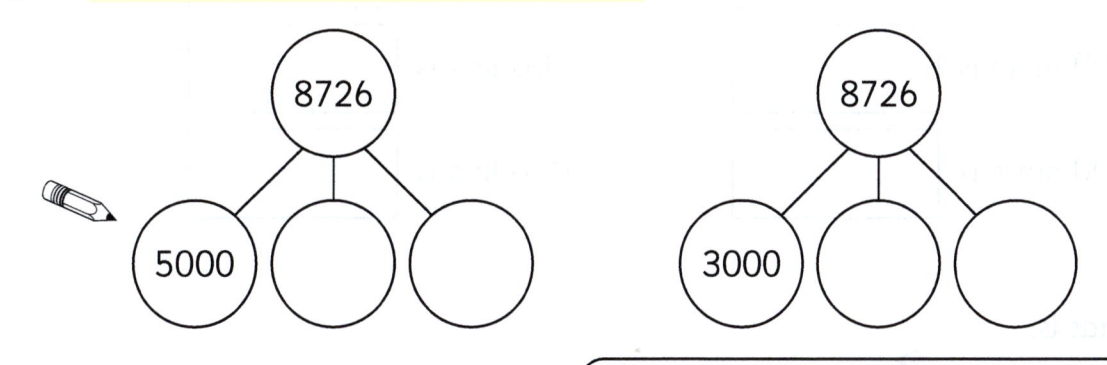

8726 → 5000, ☐, ☐

8726 → 3000, ☐, ☐

Is there more than one right answer? Compare with a partner.

Problem Solving and Reasoning

3) Ajit and Nicole are thinking of different 4-digit numbers.

Ajit: "My number has five thousands."

Nicole: "My number has 48 hundreds."

Who is thinking of the bigger number? Explain your answer.

Did that go well?

Block 1 — Place Value — Step 7

1, 10, 100 and 1000 More or Less

1 Complete the sentences.

Th	H	T	O
1000 1000 1000 1000 1000	100 100 100 100 100 100 100 100 100	10	1 1 1

Use a place value chart and counters to help you.

The number shown is ☐.

1 more is ☐   1 less is ☐

10 more is ☐   10 less is ☐

100 more is ☐   100 less is ☐

1000 more is ☐   1000 less is ☐

2 What is:

10 more than 3098? ☐   100 less than 3098? ☐

Problem Solving and Reasoning

3 Write down a 4-digit number where:

Finding 1 less changes the thousands digit. ☐

Finding 10 more changes the hundreds digit. ☐

Compare your answers with a partner.

Do you need one more go at that?

Block 1 — Place Value — Step 8

Number Lines to 10 000

1 What numbers are the arrows pointing to?

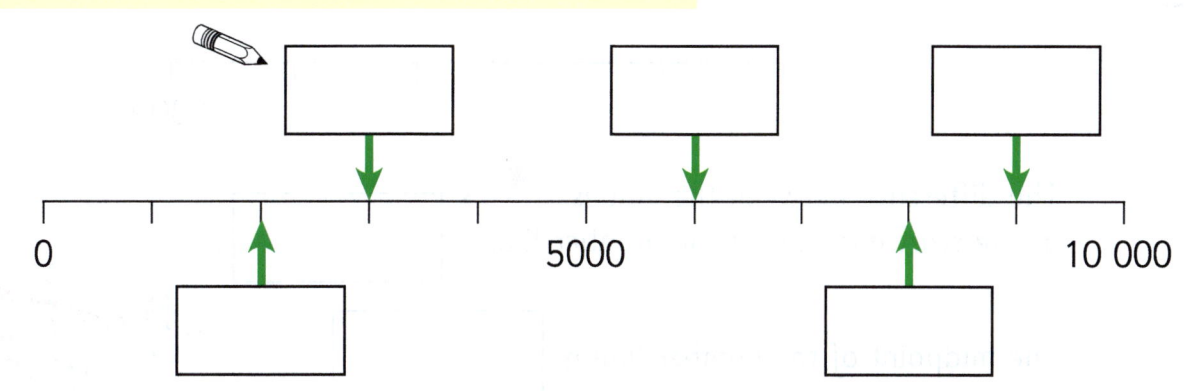

(number line from 0 to 10 000 with 5000 marked, arrows pointing to various positions)

2 Draw an arrow to show the position of 7000 on each number line.

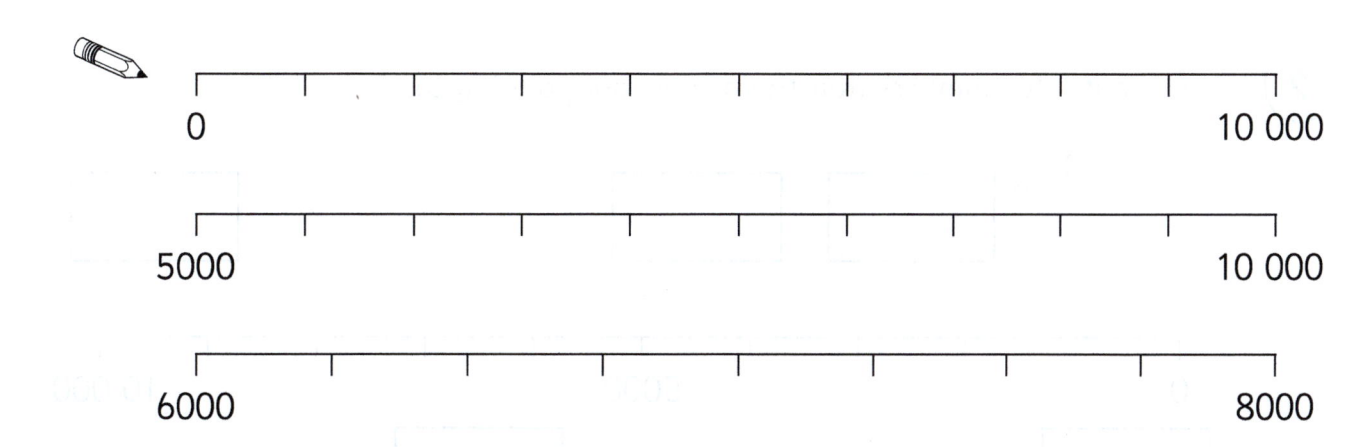

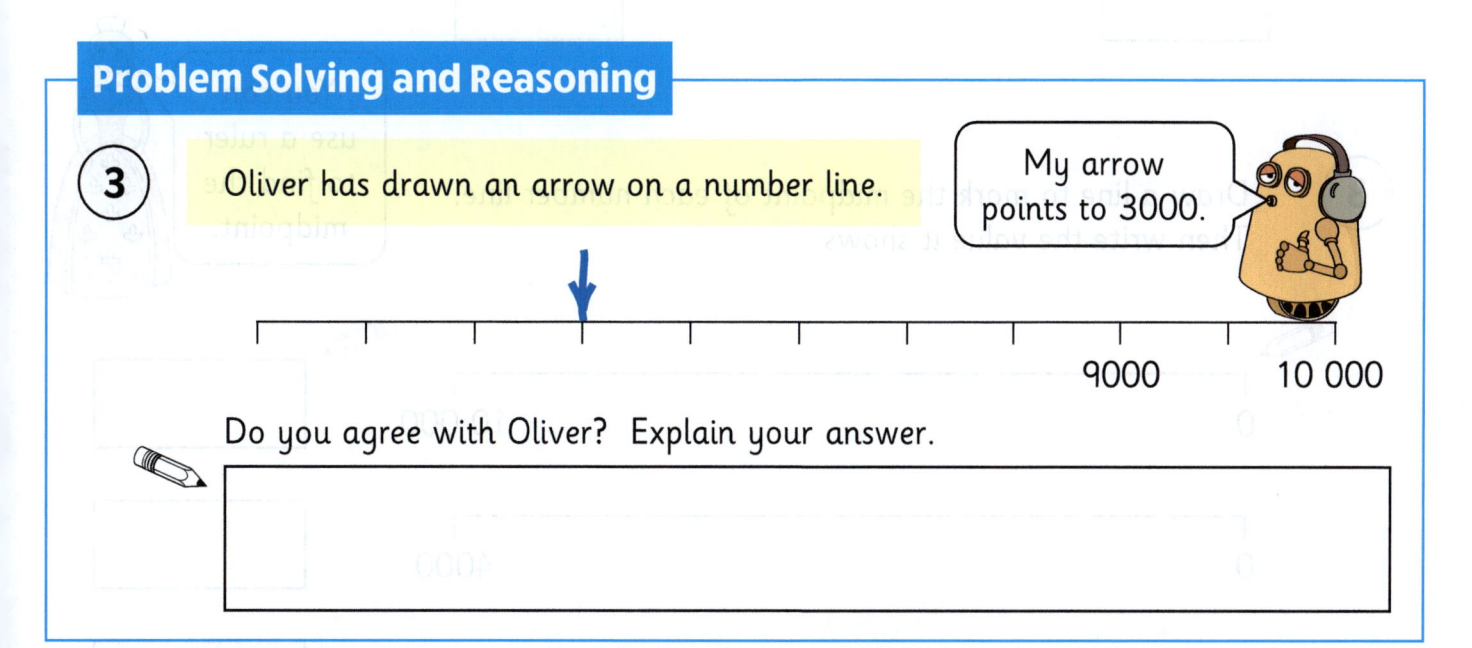

(number line from 0 to 10 000)

(number line from 5000 to 10 000)

(number line from 6000 to 8000)

Problem Solving and Reasoning

3 Oliver has drawn an arrow on a number line.

"My arrow points to 3000."

(number line showing an arrow, with 9000 and 10 000 marked)

Do you agree with Oliver? Explain your answer.

Beep, beep... all good?

Block 1 — Place Value — Step 9

Estimating on Number Lines

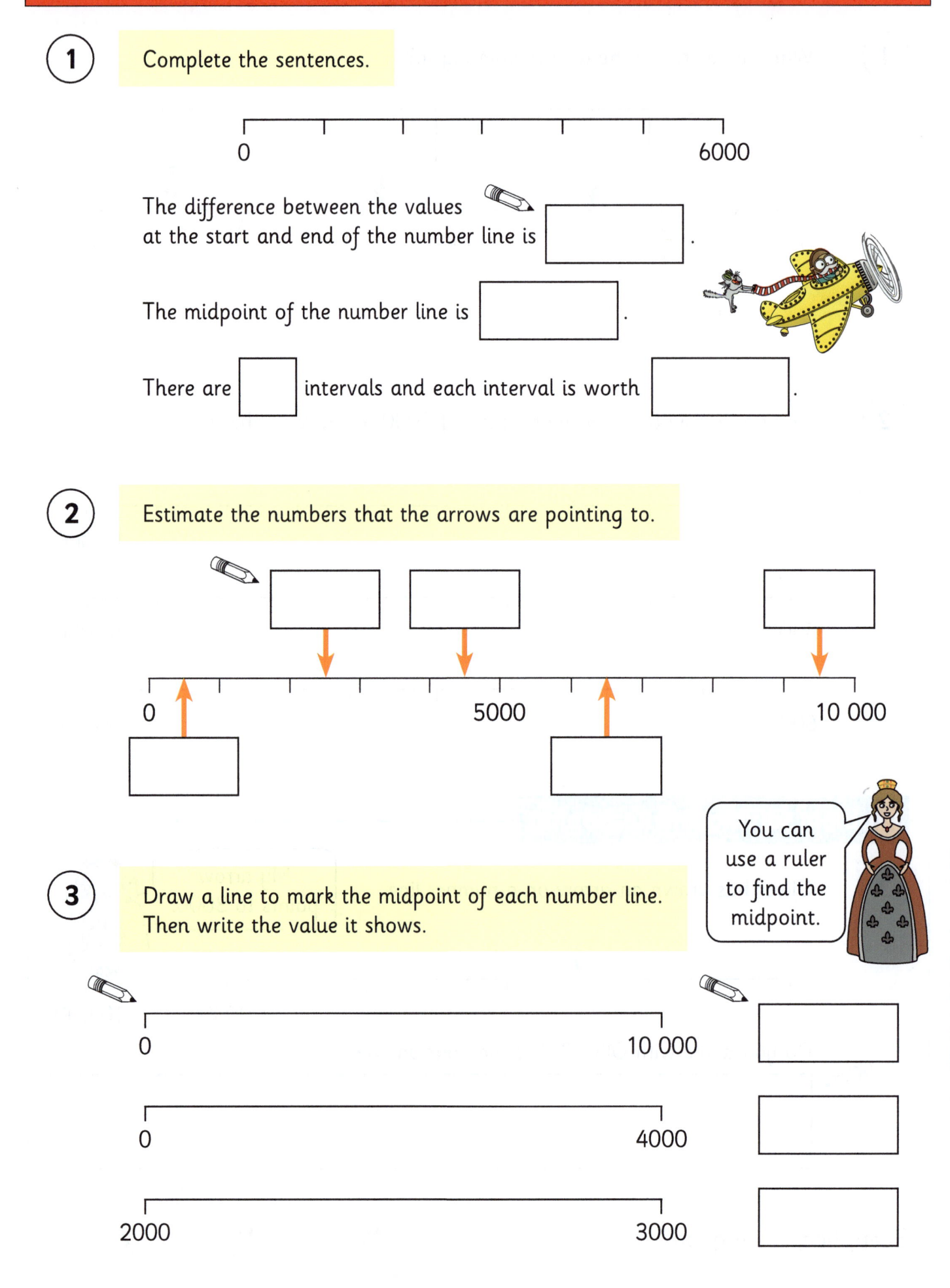

1 Complete the sentences.

0 ———————————————— 6000

The difference between the values at the start and end of the number line is ☐ .

The midpoint of the number line is ☐ .

There are ☐ intervals and each interval is worth ☐ .

2 Estimate the numbers that the arrows are pointing to.

0 ———————— 5000 ———————— 10 000

3 Draw a line to mark the midpoint of each number line. Then write the value it shows.

You can use a ruler to find the midpoint.

0 ———————————————— 10 000

0 ———————————————— 4000

2000 ———————————————— 3000

Block 1 — Place Value — Step 10

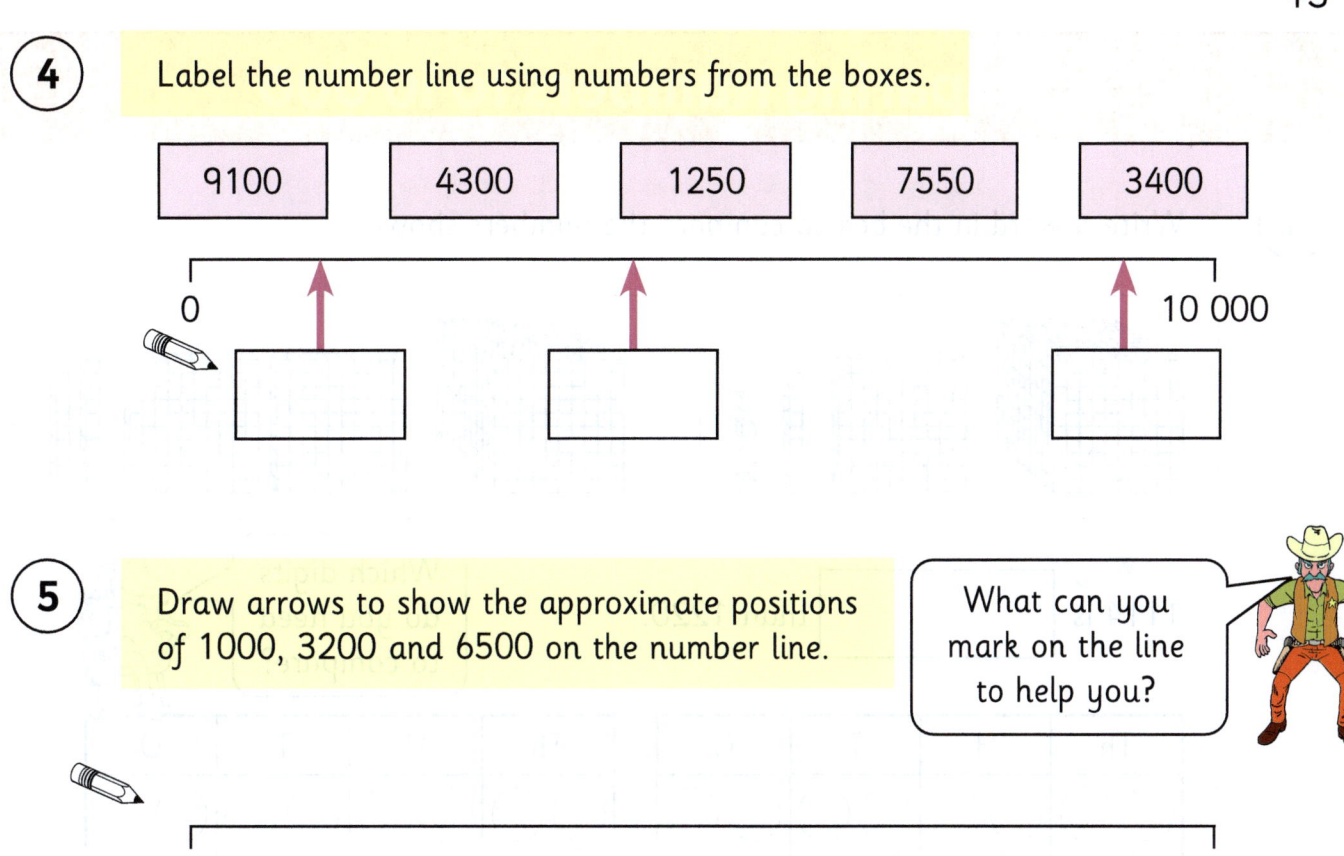

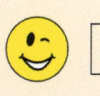

④ Label the number line using numbers from the boxes.

| 9100 | 4300 | 1250 | 7550 | 3400 |

0 ──────────────────────────────── 10 000

⑤ Draw arrows to show the approximate positions of 1000, 3200 and 6500 on the number line.

What can you mark on the line to help you?

0 ──────────────────────────────── 10 000

Problem Solving and Reasoning

⑥ Three points have been marked on the number line.

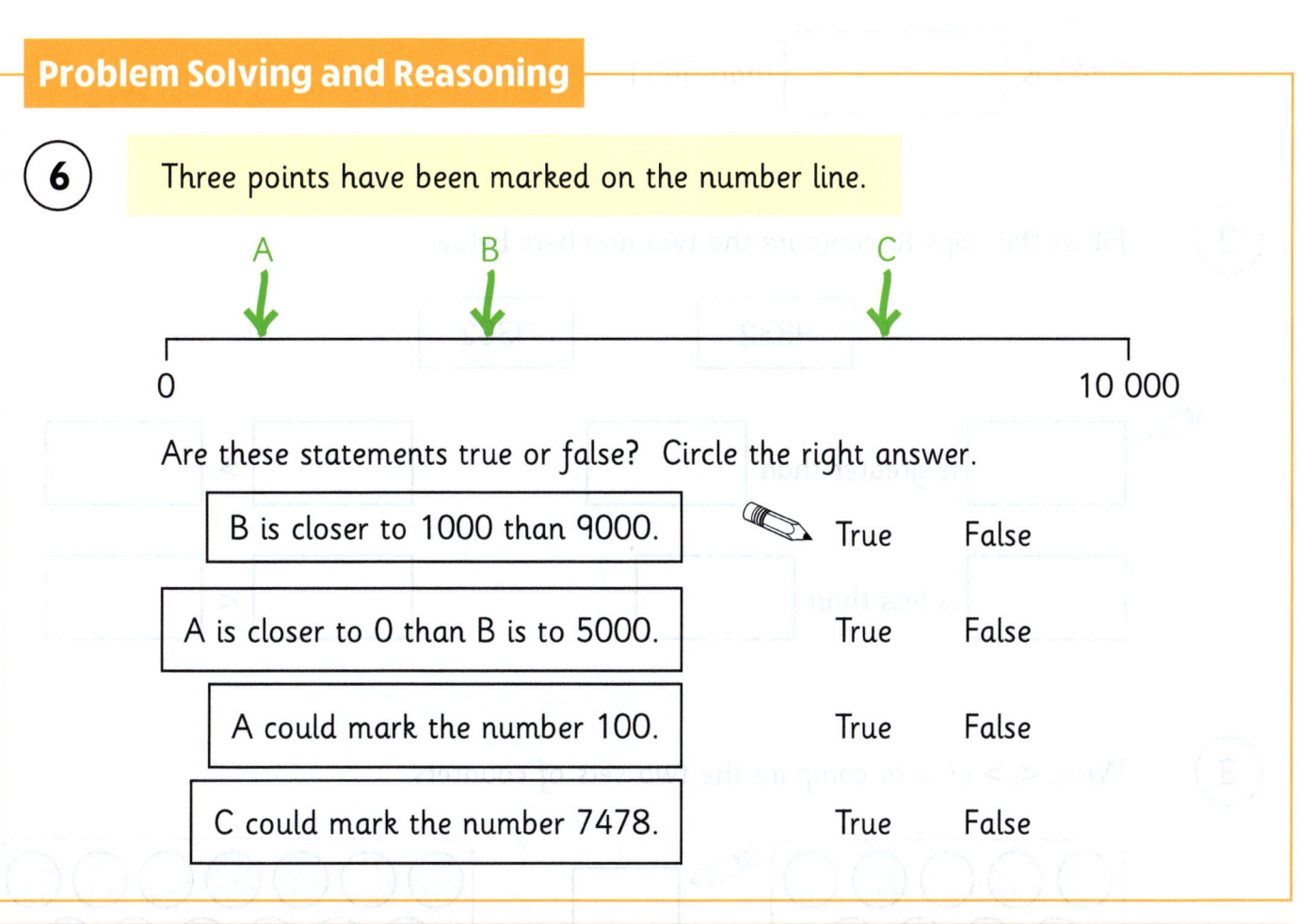

A   B   C
↓   ↓   ↓
0 ──────────────────────────────── 10 000

Are these statements true or false? Circle the right answer.

B is closer to 1000 than 9000.	True False
A is closer to 0 than B is to 5000.	True False
A could mark the number 100.	True False
C could mark the number 7478.	True False

How well do you estimate that went?

Block 1 — Place Value — Step 10

Comparing Numbers to 10 000

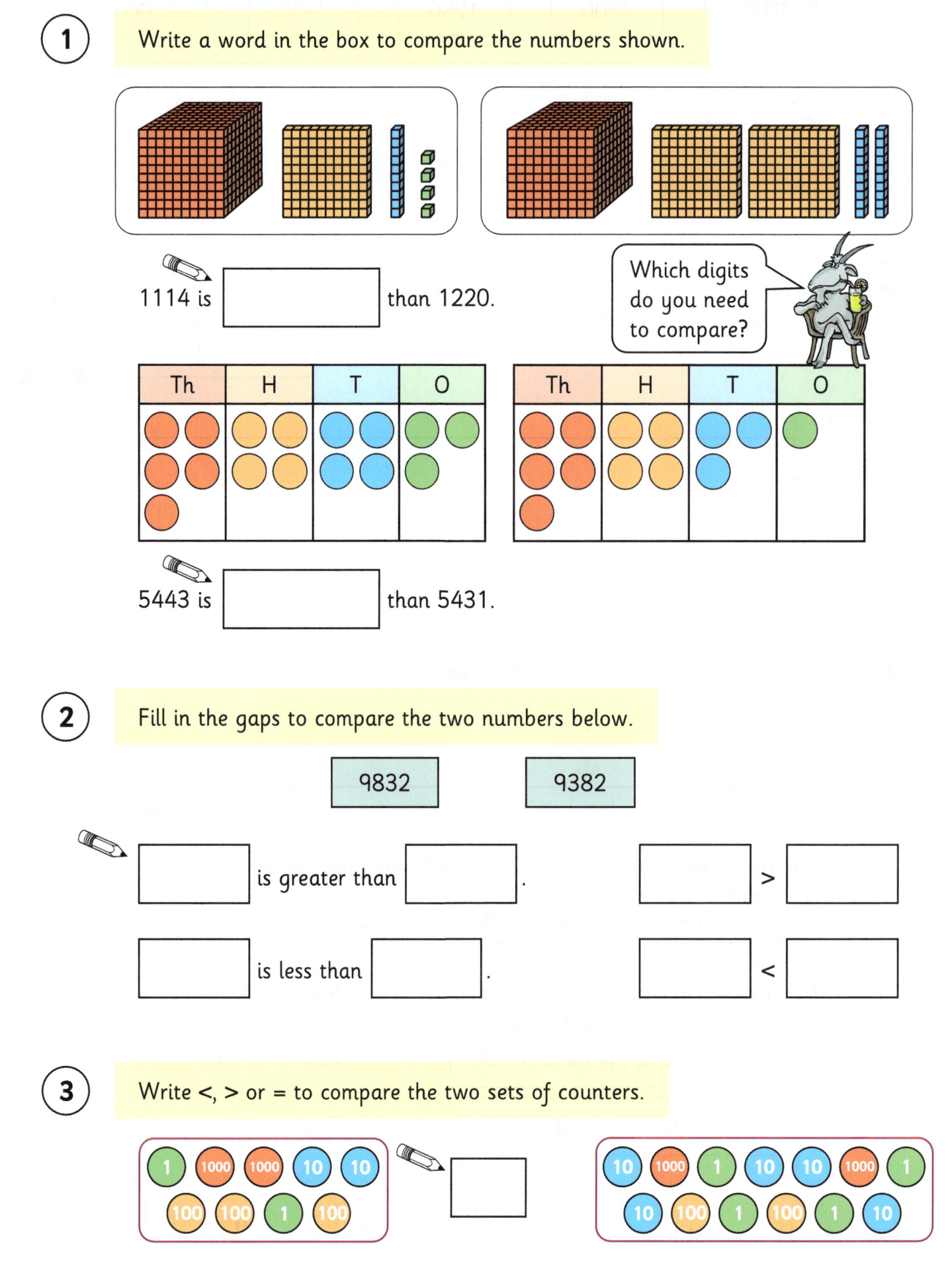

1 Write a word in the box to compare the numbers shown.

1114 is [ ] than 1220.

Which digits do you need to compare?

5443 is [ ] than 5431.

2 Fill in the gaps to compare the two numbers below.

9832   9382

[ ] is greater than [ ].   [ ] > [ ]

[ ] is less than [ ].   [ ] < [ ]

3 Write <, > or = to compare the two sets of counters.

Block 1 — Place Value — Step 11

4 Which cake is heavier? Circle your answer.

2402 g

2420 g

5 Write < or > to compare the numbers.

2198 ☐ 6000   9752 ☐ 7952

1209 ☐ 988   259 ☐ 2590

7089 ☐ 7300   1008 ☐ 1080

1568 ☐ 1586   9753 ☐ 9375

Problem Solving and Reasoning

6 Yasmin has written a correct statement in her book. She has dripped her lunch onto it.

The sauce has covered the same digit in both numbers.

58☐4 < 5☐84

The missing digit must be a 9.

Do you agree with Yasmin? Explain your answer.

Was that greater than or less than okay?

Block 1 — Place Value — Step 11

Ordering Numbers to 10 000

1 The diagrams show three different numbers.
Write the numbers in order from smallest to greatest.

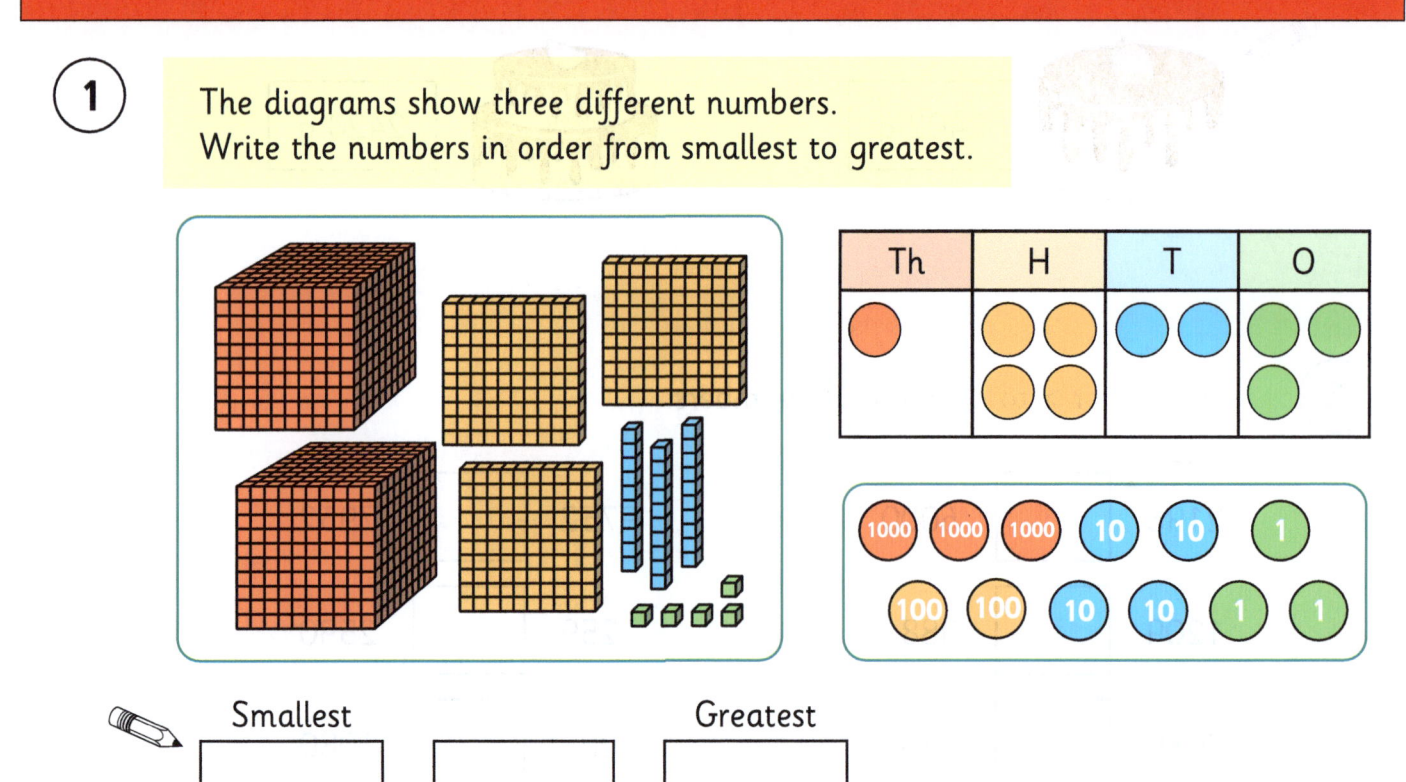

Smallest ☐ , ☐ , ☐ Greatest

2 Write the prices of these holidays in order from most expensive to least expensive.

Holiday	Price
Greek Islands Tour	£2549
Luxury Lake District Adventure	£689
Kangaroo Caper	£4859
Bognor Regis by Bus	£1439

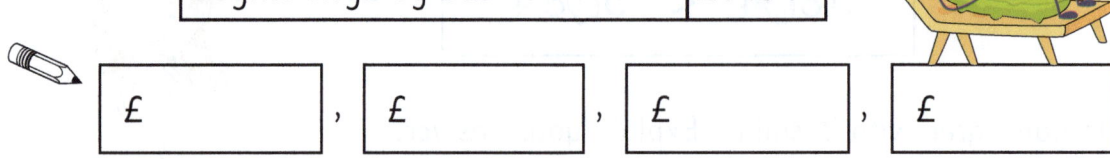

£ ☐ , £ ☐ , £ ☐ , £ ☐

3 Write these numbers in ascending order: 6580, 3050, 980

☐ , ☐ , ☐

Block 1 — Place Value — Step 12

4 Write these numbers in descending order: 5324, 5432, 5423

☐ , ☐ , ☐

5 Write a number in each box to make these statements true.

5320 < ☐ < 6320

985 < ☐ < 9806

5320 > ☐ > 5310

2400 > ☐ > 240

Look carefully at the inequality signs.

Is there more than one right answer?

Problem Solving and Reasoning

6 The Rock Bottom music shop has these instruments for sale.

Trumpet

Guitar £4950

Violin

The trumpet is more expensive than the guitar.

The violin costs less than £3000.

The trumpet is twice the price of the violin.

All instruments cost a whole number of pounds.

How much could the trumpet cost? Give two possible answers.

£ ☐   £ ☐

Have you got all that in order?

Block 1 — Place Value — Step 12

Roman Numerals

1 Draw lines to match the Roman numerals to the right numbers.

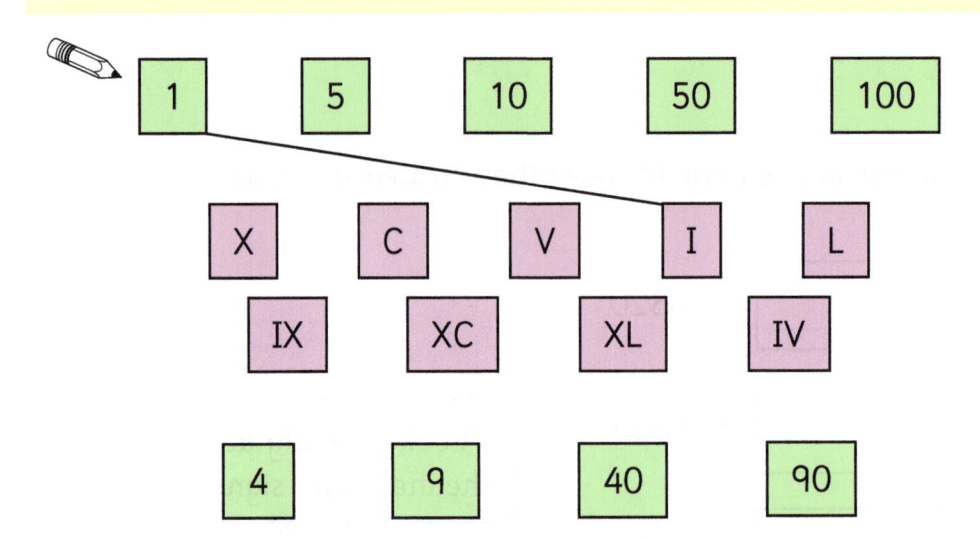

| 1 | 5 | 10 | 50 | 100 |

| X | C | V | I | L |

| IX | XC | XL | IV |

| 4 | 9 | 40 | 90 |

2 Write the number shown by the Roman numerals.

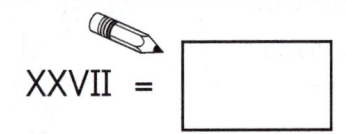

XXVII = ☐   LXXV = ☐

LV = ☐   LXXXII = ☐

XLVI = ☐   XCIX = ☐

Is it easier to write LXXXX or XC?

3 Write each of these numbers in Roman numerals.

21 = ☐   91 = ☐

32 = ☐   84 = ☐

64 = ☐   49 = ☐

4 Complete these additions. Write your answers in Roman numerals.

I + I = ☐   V + V = ☐

L + L = ☐   IV + VI = ☐

XV + LV = ☐   LX + XL = ☐

Problem Solving and Reasoning

5 Tom is reading a number written in Roman numerals.

XCIX

"The number is 121."

Explain Tom's mistake.

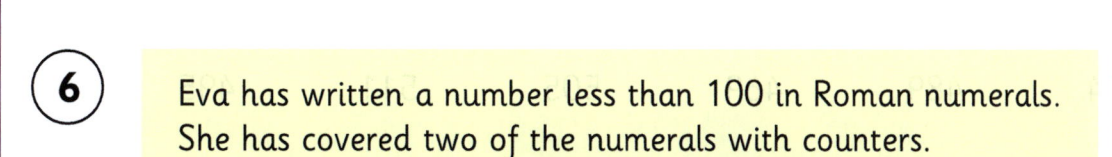

6 Eva has written a number less than 100 in Roman numerals. She has covered two of the numerals with counters.

● C V ● I I

Work out the missing Roman numerals.

☐ C V ☐ I I

Explain how you know.

Did you conquer Roman numerals?

Block 1 — Place Value — Step 13

Rounding to the Nearest 10

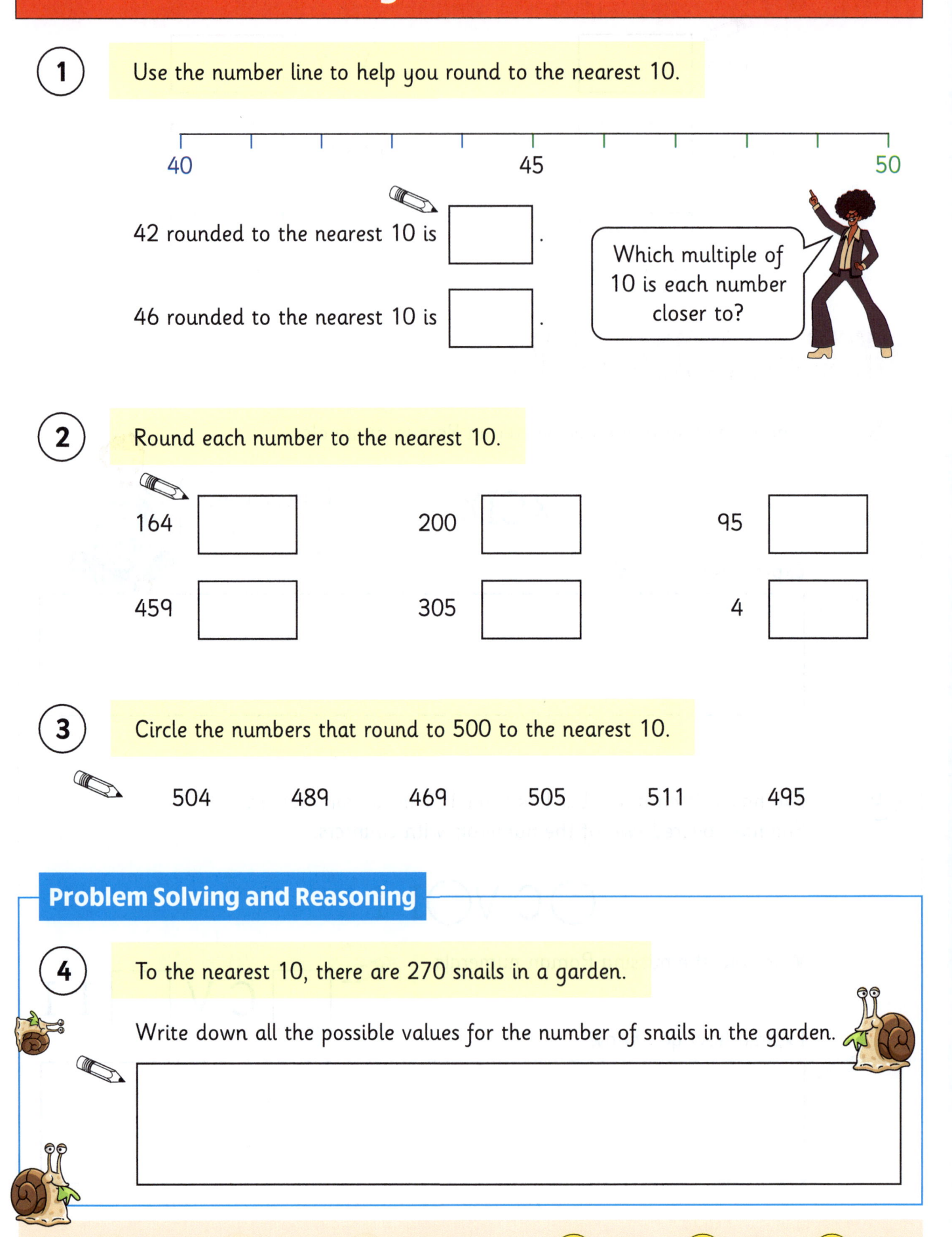

1   Use the number line to help you round to the nearest 10.

40 — 45 — 50

42 rounded to the nearest 10 is ☐.

46 rounded to the nearest 10 is ☐.

Which multiple of 10 is each number closer to?

2   Round each number to the nearest 10.

164 ☐   200 ☐   95 ☐

459 ☐   305 ☐   4 ☐

3   Circle the numbers that round to 500 to the nearest 10.

504   489   469   505   511   495

Problem Solving and Reasoning

4   To the nearest 10, there are 270 snails in a garden.

Write down all the possible values for the number of snails in the garden.

Have you got your head round rounding?

Block 1 — Place Value — Step 14

Rounding to the Nearest 100

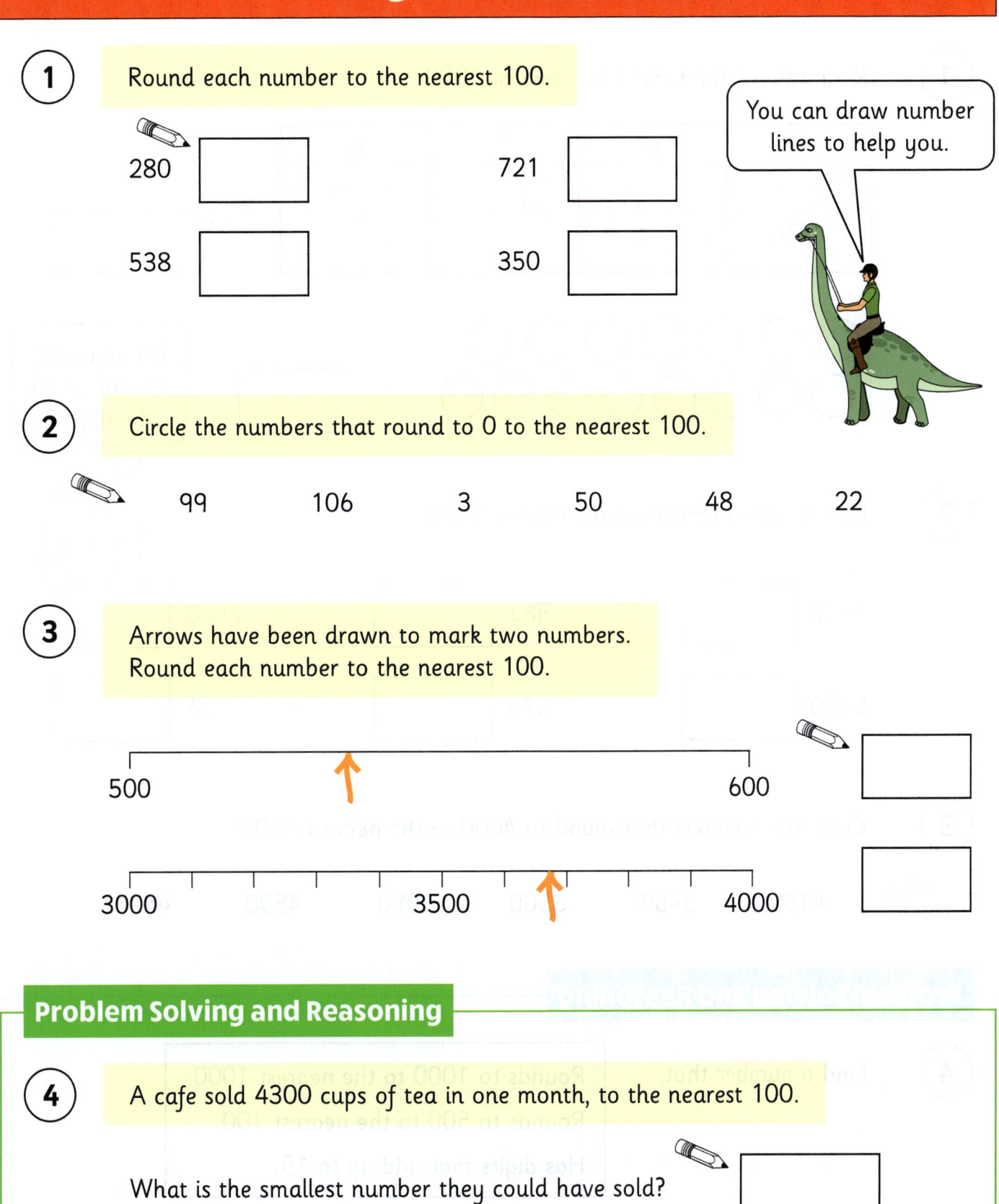

1 Round each number to the nearest 100.

280 ☐   721 ☐

538 ☐   350 ☐

You can draw number lines to help you.

2 Circle the numbers that round to 0 to the nearest 100.

99   106   3   50   48   22

3 Arrows have been drawn to mark two numbers. Round each number to the nearest 100.

500 —————↑————————————— 600   ☐

3000 ———————3500———↑———4000   ☐

Problem Solving and Reasoning

4 A cafe sold 4300 cups of tea in one month, to the nearest 100.

What is the smallest number they could have sold?   ☐

What is the greatest number they could have sold?   ☐

Did you get all that?

Block 1 — Place Value — Step 15

Rounding to the Nearest 1000

1 Round these numbers to the nearest 1000.

Th	H	T	O

Do you need to look at all the digits?

2 Round these numbers to the nearest 1000.

1897 ☐   582 ☐   7500 ☐

5400 ☐   470 ☐   24 ☐

3 Circle the numbers that round to 4000 to the nearest 1000.

4150   3459   3500   3980   4500   4495

Problem Solving and Reasoning

4 Find a number that:

Rounds to 1000 to the nearest 1000.
Rounds to 500 to the nearest 100.
Has digits that add up to 15.

Give three possible answers.   ☐   ☐   ☐

Can you round to the nearest 1000?

Block 1 — Place Value — Step 16

Rounding to the Nearest 10, 100 or 1000

1 Round this number to the nearest 10, the nearest 100 and the nearest 1000.

Th	H	T	O
●●● ●●	●●●	●●● ●●●	●

To the nearest 10:

To the nearest 100:

To the nearest 1000:

2 Fill in the gaps in the table.

	6491	8555	452
To the nearest 10	6490		
To the nearest 100			
To the nearest 1000			

Problem Solving and Reasoning

3 There were 7948 people at a pancake flipping competition.

Round the number of people to...

the nearest 10:

the nearest 100:

the nearest 1000:

Which do you think is the most sensible way of rounding the number? Explain your answer.

Did you catch that?

Block 1 — Place Value — Step 17

Block 2 — Addition and Subtraction

Mental Adding and Subtracting

1 Work out the calculations. Use the place value chart on the right to help you.

Th	H	T	O
●●● ●		●●●	●●●●

3134 − 100 =

3134 − 3000 =

3134 + 60 =

3134 + 5 =

2 Use this fact to work out the calculations below.   45 + 80 = 125

450 + 800 =

1250 − 800 =

3 There are 8053 ants in a colony. 700 ants leave, then 40 ants return.

How many ants are there now?

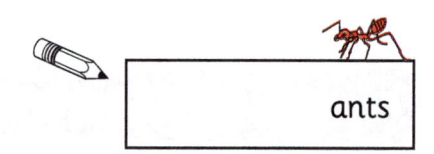

_____ ants

Problem Solving and Reasoning

4 Antoinette subtracted 200 from a 4-digit number.

"I only had to change the number in the hundreds column."

Using an example 4-digit number, explain why this is not always true.

How is your mental adding and subtracting?

Block 2 — Addition and Subtraction — Step 1

Adding Numbers with No Exchanges

1) Write the addition shown by the place value chart, then work out the answer.

Which of the columns should you add first?

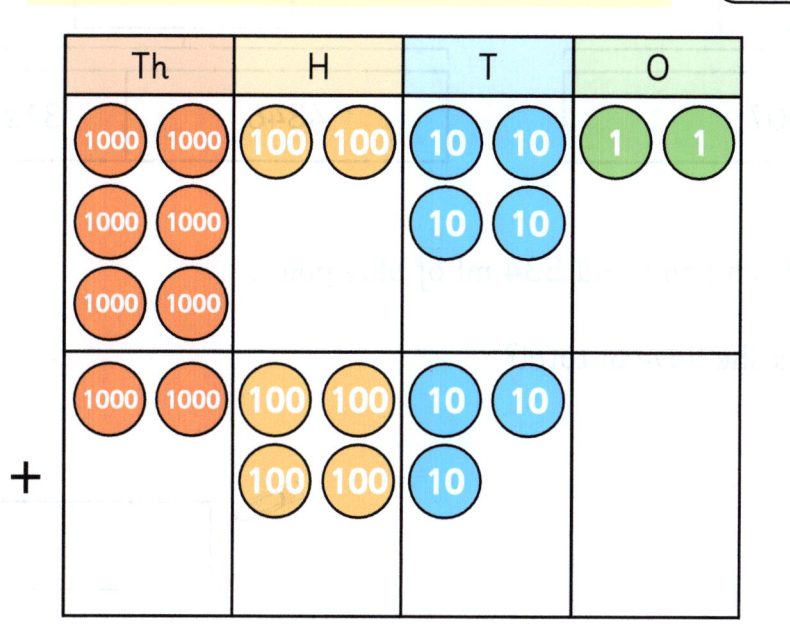

2) Work out these additions.

```
  1 4 0 3
+ 6 4 3 5
---------
```

```
  2 1 6 5
+ 7 6 0 4
---------
```

3) What is:

7561 + 1033?

3042 + 5916?

Block 2 — Addition and Subtraction — Step 2

4 Use addition to find the missing numbers on these bar models.

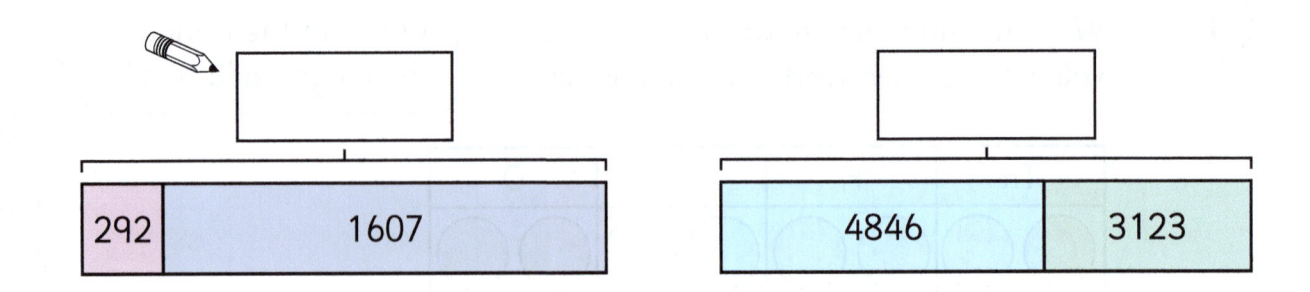

| 292 | 1607 |

| 4846 | 3123 |

5 Erica has 3065 ml of red paint and 534 ml of blue paint.

How much paint does she have in total?

☐ ml

Problem Solving and Reasoning

6 Talat covers some numbers on the right. His addition gives the largest possible answer where there are no exchanges.

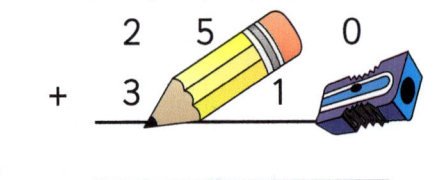

```
  2 ▨ 5 ▨ 0
+ 3 ▨ 1 ▨
—————————
```

Which two 4-digit numbers are being added?

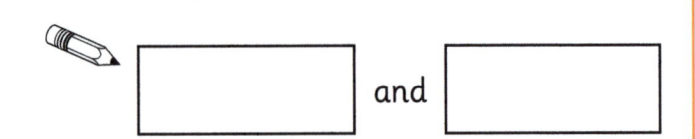

☐ and ☐

7 Work out the missing digits in the calculation and fill in the bar model to show the same information.

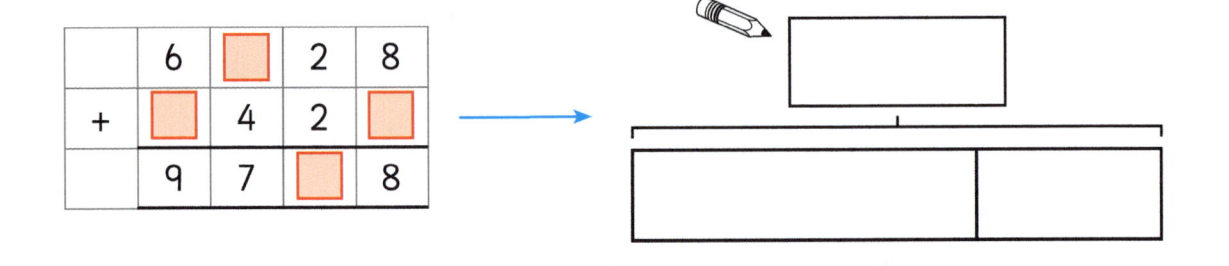

```
   6 ▢ 2 8
 + ▢ 4 2 ▢
 ————————
   9 7 ▢ 8
```

Can you add numbers with no exchanges?

Block 2 — Addition and Subtraction — Step 2

Adding Numbers with One Exchange

1 Work out these additions.

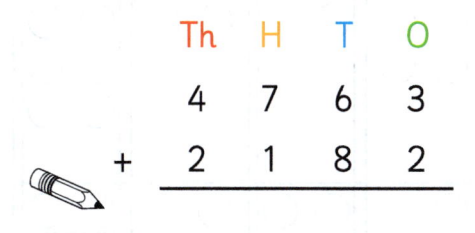

```
  Th  H  T  O           Th  H  T  O
   4  7  6  3            5  3  1  2
+  2  1  8  2         +  1  9  0  6
  _____           _____
```

You can use counters and a place value chart to help.

2 Fill in the missing number in each part-whole model.

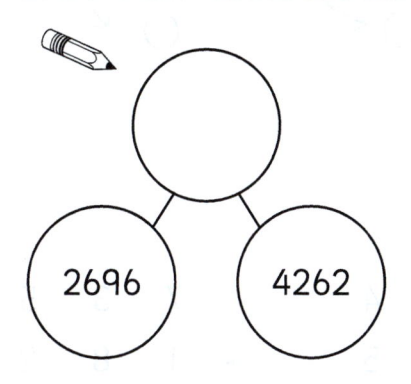

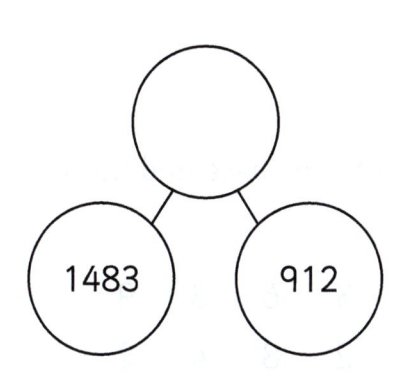

2696   4262

1483   912

3 Work out the sum of 3268 and 4831.

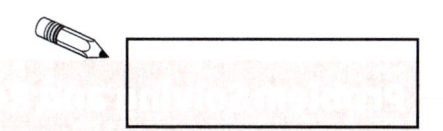

Problem Solving and Reasoning

4 Maria adds 372 to a number to give 7546.

Complete her addition and find her original number.

Her original number was: ☐

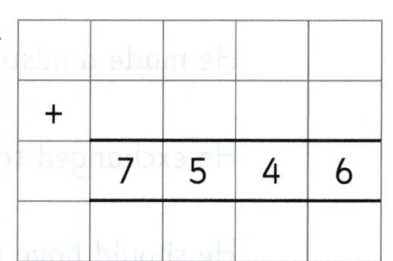

```
+
       7  5  4  6
```

Are you OK adding with one exchange?

Block 2 — Addition and Subtraction — Step 3

Adding Numbers with More Exchanges

1 Use the place value chart on the right to help you answer the addition.

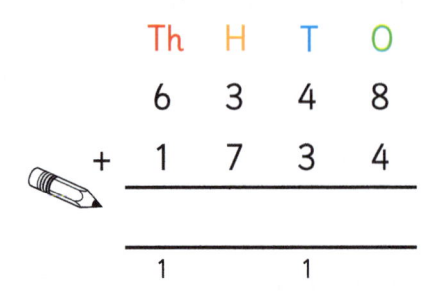

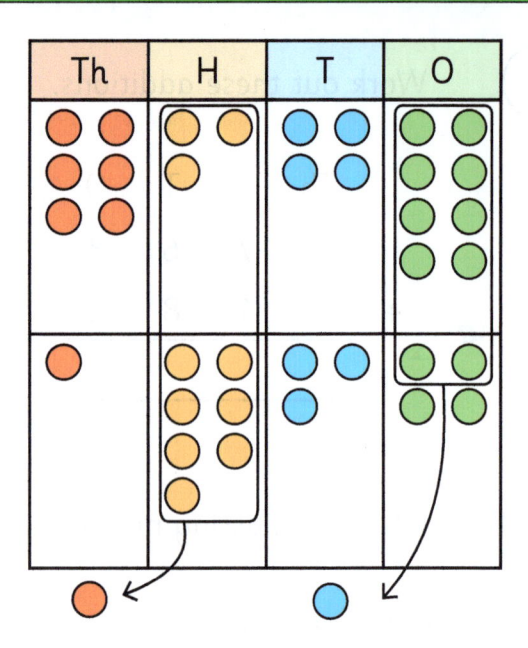

```
  Th  H  T  O
   6  3  4  8
+  1  7  3  4
  _____
      1     1
```

2 Work out these additions.

```
   3 6 3 9        8 1 6 4        7 3 5 5
+  2 8 4 2     +    9 4 5     +  1 8 2 7
```

Problem Solving and Reasoning

3 Felix works out the addition on the right.

```
  Th  H  T  O
   3  6  5  8
+  1  5  4  4
  _____
   5  1  9  2
      1     1
```

Tick the statements below that are true.

He made a mistake in the tens column. ☐

He exchanged ten hundreds for a thousand. ☐

He should have made one exchange only. ☐

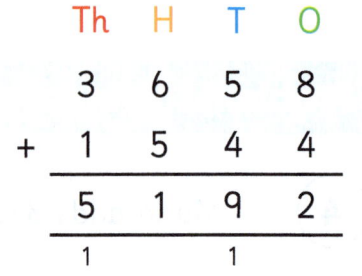

How did you manage with more exchanges?

Block 2 — Addition and Subtraction — Step 4

Subtracting Numbers with No Exchanges

1) Write the subtraction shown below and work out the answer.

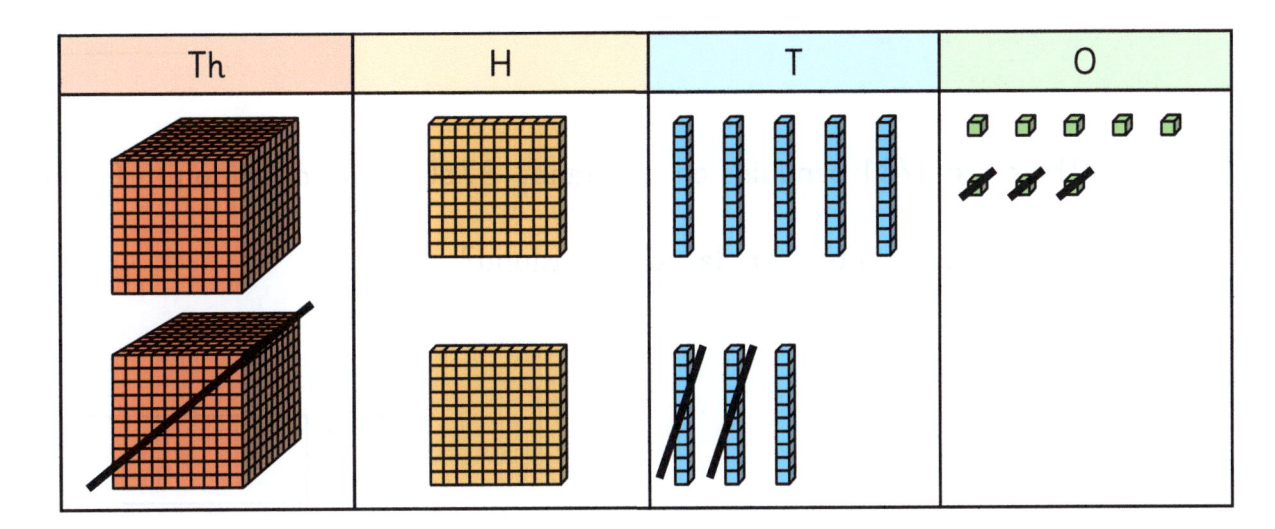

Th	H	T	O

Discuss why you don't need to make an exchange in any column.

	Th	H	T	O
	2	2	8	8
−				

2) Fill in the missing numbers on each bar model.

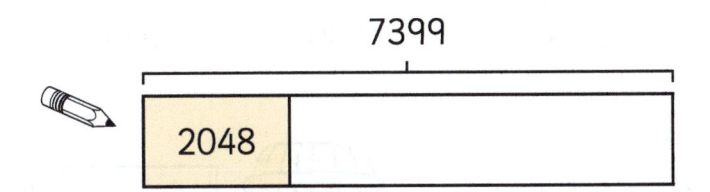

7399
| 2048 | |

9738
| | 6024 |

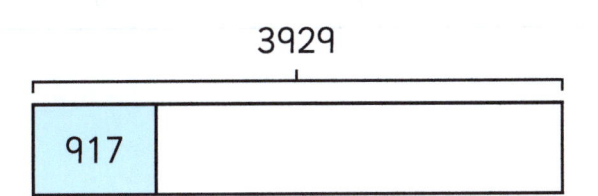

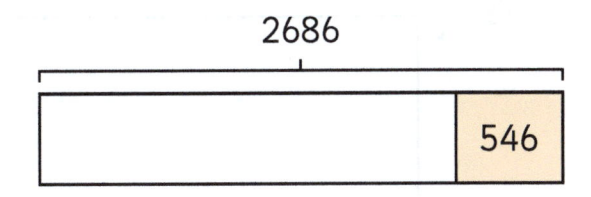

3929
| 917 | |

2686
| | 546 |

Block 2 — Addition and Subtraction — Step 5

3 Work out the difference between 6385 and 7488.

4 There are 9781 penguins on an island. 3760 go on a holiday to Egypt.

How many penguins are left on the island?

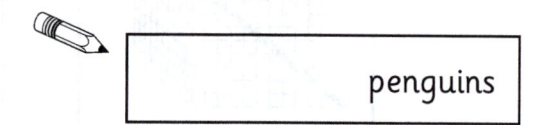

_____ penguins

Problem Solving and Reasoning

5 Shreena shows a number using place value counters.

Th	H	T	O
1000 1000	100 100	10 10	1
1000		10	

Circle the numbers she can subtract from her number that would have no exchanges.

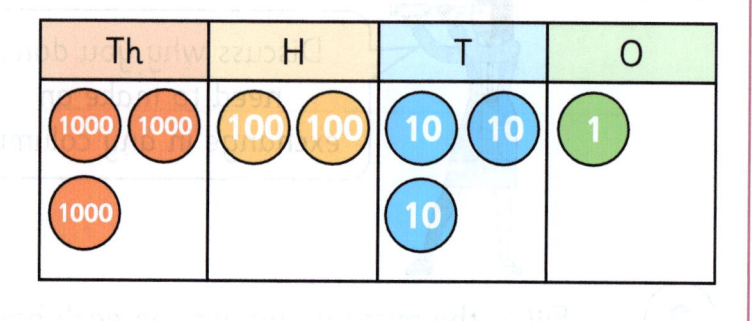

2210   1040   3134   1230   311

6 George needs 6500 ml of water for a fish tank. He buys the barrel on the right, but finds the barrel has 2120 ml less water than it should.

Contains: 8645 ml of water

Does the barrel still have enough water for the fish tank? Show your working.

Is subtracting with no exchanges all fine?

Block 2 — Addition and Subtraction — Step 5

Subtracting Numbers with One Exchange

1 Use the place value chart on the right to help you answer the subtraction.

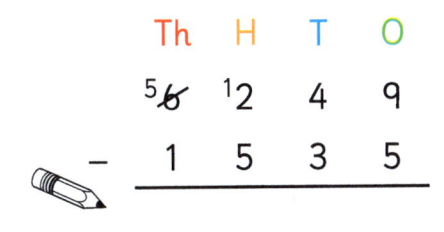

```
   Th  H  T  O
   ⁵6̶ ¹2  4  9
 -  1  5  3  5
   _____
```

2 Work out these subtractions.

8	6	7	1
- 4	6	2	8

4	5	4	9
- 3	7	1	2

9	9	0	3
-	8	6	1

3 Oscar had 4274 social media followers. After sharing a video, he now has 5319 followers.

How many followers did he gain?

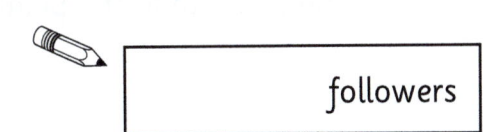

_____ followers

Problem Solving and Reasoning

4 Fill in the missing numbers so that both subtractions give the same answer.

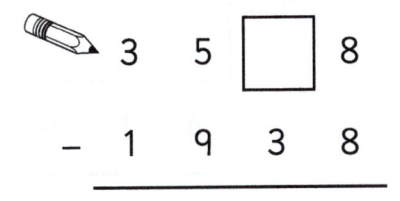

```
   3  5  ☐  8
 - 1  9  3  8
   _____
```

```
   4  3  3  ☐
 - ☐  7  1  2
   _____
```

Subtracting Numbers with More Exchanges

1 Work out 5221 − 3416. Use the place value chart to help you exchange.

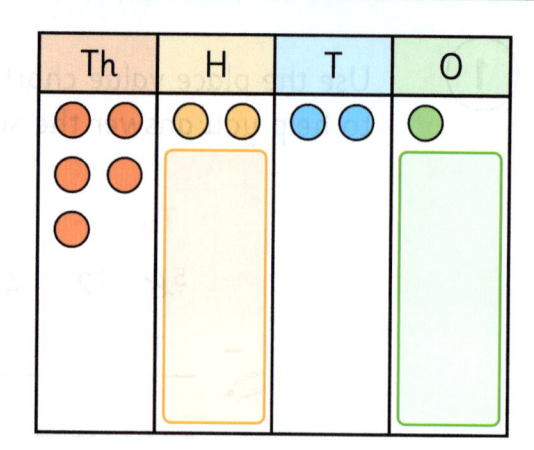

```
  Th  H  T  O
   5  2  2  1
 − 3  4  1  6
 ───────────
```

Th	H	T	O

2 Fill in the missing number in each part-whole model.

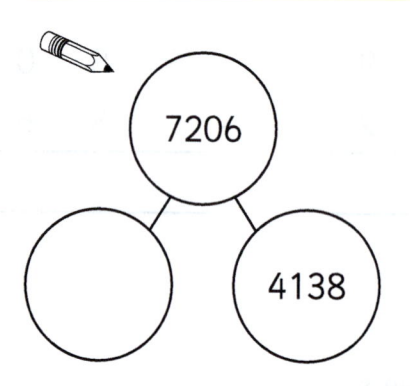

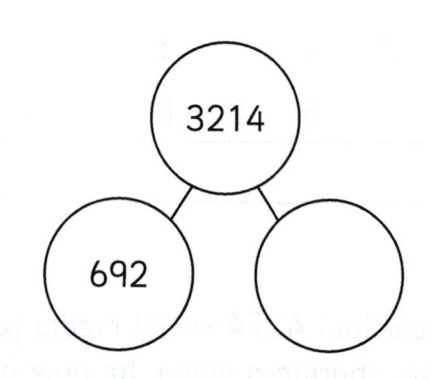

7206 → ( ), 4138

3214 → 692, ( )

3 How much more does the ring cost than the painting?

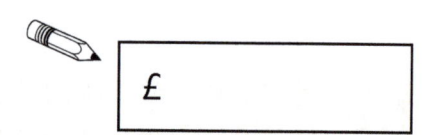

Ring: £8240   Painting: £5319

£ _____

Problem Solving and Reasoning

4 Find a number that can go in the red box.

- The result of the calculation must be a 3-digit number.
- The subtraction must have exactly two exchanges.

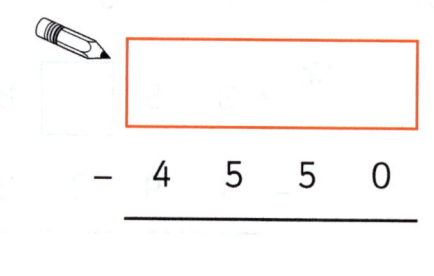

```
   [    ]
 −  4 5 5 0
 ─────────
```

Can you manage lots of exchanges?

Subtracting Efficiently

1) Work out these subtractions.

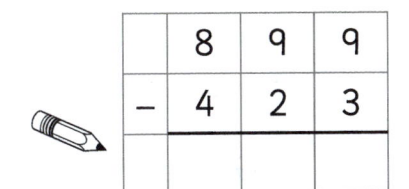

	8	9	9
−	4	2	3

	9	0	0
−	4	2	4

What do you notice? Which calculation was easier to do?

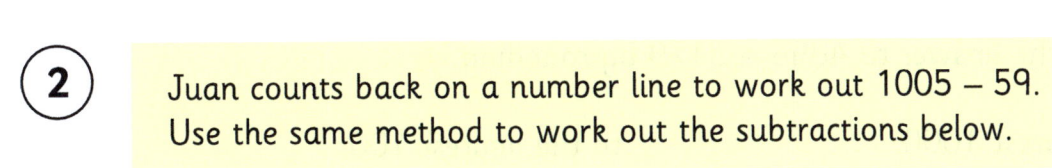

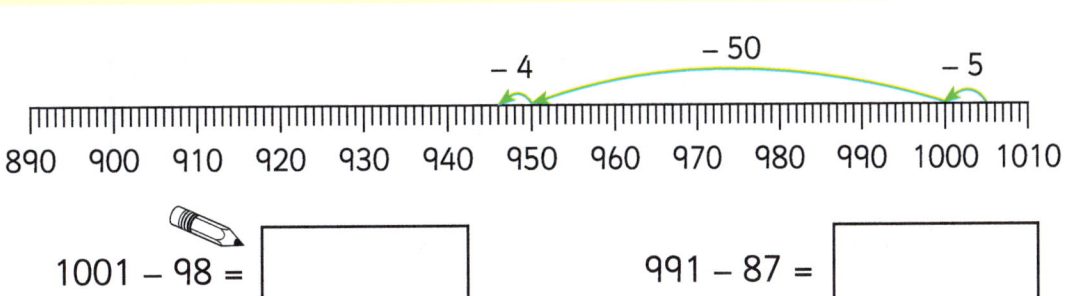

2) Juan counts back on a number line to work out 1005 − 59. Use the same method to work out the subtractions below.

(number line from 890 to 1010, showing −5, −50, −4)

1001 − 98 = ☐

991 − 87 = ☐

3) Fill in the missing numbers.

1105 − 998 = 1107 − ☐ , so 1105 − 998 = ☐

Problem Solving and Reasoning

4) Fallon tries to work out 5001 − 1782 using a written method.

Give an easier subtraction she can do (with no exchanges) and find the answer.

```
    5  0  0  1
  − 1  7  8  2
  _____
```
→
```
    −
  _____
```

Can you spot ways to subtract efficiently?

Block 2 — Addition and Subtraction — Step 8

Estimating Answers

1 Decide whether the estimated answer would be greater than or less than the actual answer. Circle your answer.

678 + 199 ⟶ 700 + 200   Greater than / Less than

3102 + 704 ⟶ 3000 + 700   Greater than / Less than

2 Estimate the answer to 4895 + 3179 by rounding:

to the nearest 1000.   to the nearest 100.

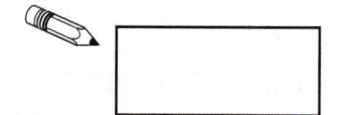

3 Child bicycles cost £148. Adult bicycles cost £397.

Estimate the total cost of one child bicycle and one adult bicycle.

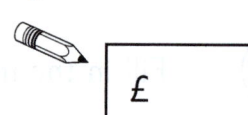

£ _____

Problem Solving and Reasoning

4 Leon estimates the answer to 6789 − 2082 in three different ways:

A: 7000 − 2000   B: 6800 − 2100   C: 6790 − 2080

Find the difference between each estimate and the actual answer.

Which estimate is closest? Which calculation is easiest to do?

Are you excellent at estimating?

Block 2 — Addition and Subtraction — Step 9

Strategies for Checking Answers

1 Circle the correct word in each sentence.

Addition is the (inverse / estimated) operation of subtraction.

(Subtraction / Addition) can be done in any order.

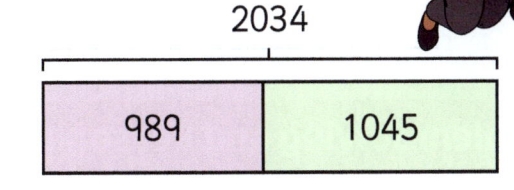

What strategies can you use to check answers?

2 Tick the correct number sentences that are shown by the bar model.

2034
989	1045

989 + 1045 = 2034 ☐   989 + 2034 = 1045 ☐

1045 − 989 = 2034 ☐   2034 − 989 = 1045 ☐

3 Write a suitable addition you could use to check each subtraction.

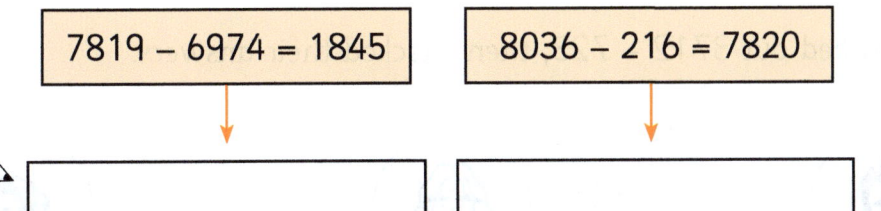

7819 − 6974 = 1845   8036 − 216 = 7820   4163 − 3998 = 165

☐   ☐   ☐

4 Draw lines to match each calculation on the top to an inverse calculation on the bottom that could be used to check the answer.

1900 + 400   230 − 190   400 + 1500   190 − 40

2300 − 1900   190 + 40   40 + 150   1900 − 400

Block 2 — Addition and Subtraction — Step 10

36

5 Write an inverse calculation and use it to check the answer to each calculation.

The difference between 1249 and 6740 is 5491.

The sum of 1249 and 6740 is 7989.

Problem Solving and Reasoning

6 Use estimation to show why the part-whole model below is not correct.

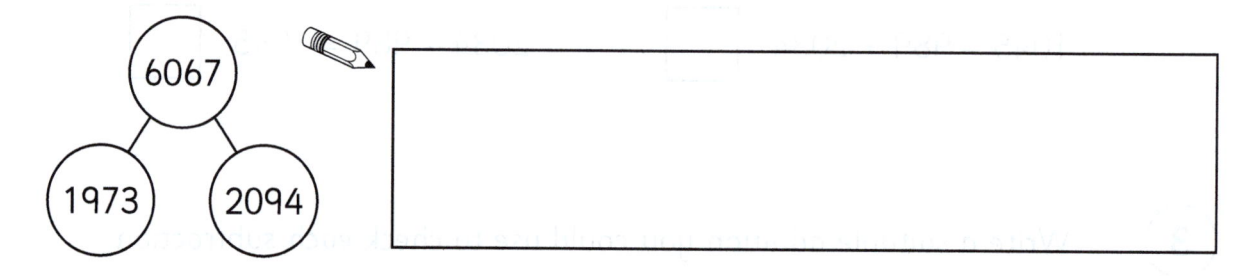

6067
1973 2094

7 Three friends worked out 3712 − 723, then checked their answers.

"I added my answer to 723."
Adam

"I did the same subtraction twice."
Beth

"I rounded each number to the nearest 100."
Colt

For each person, explain if they have used a correct strategy for checking.

Are you confident checking your answers?

Block 2 — Addition and Subtraction — Step 10

Block 3 — Area

Area

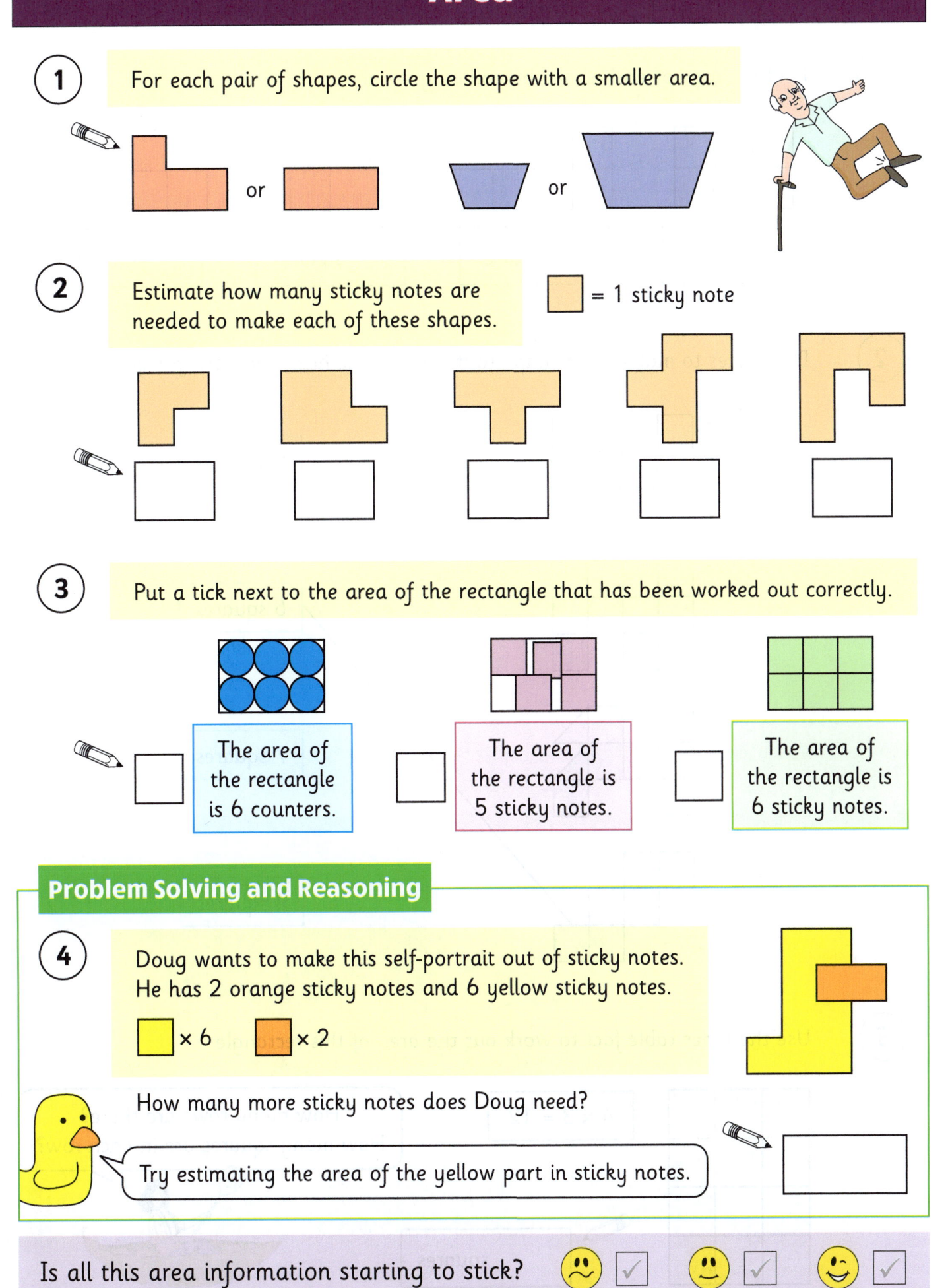

1 For each pair of shapes, circle the shape with a smaller area.

or   or

2 Estimate how many sticky notes are needed to make each of these shapes.   = 1 sticky note

3 Put a tick next to the area of the rectangle that has been worked out correctly.

☐ The area of the rectangle is 6 counters.

☐ The area of the rectangle is 5 sticky notes.

☐ The area of the rectangle is 6 sticky notes.

Problem Solving and Reasoning

4 Doug wants to make this self-portrait out of sticky notes. He has 2 orange sticky notes and 6 yellow sticky notes.

☐ × 6   ☐ × 2

How many more sticky notes does Doug need?

Try estimating the area of the yellow part in sticky notes.

Is all this area information starting to stick?

Block 3 — Area — Step 1

Counting Squares

1 Find the area of each shape by counting squares.

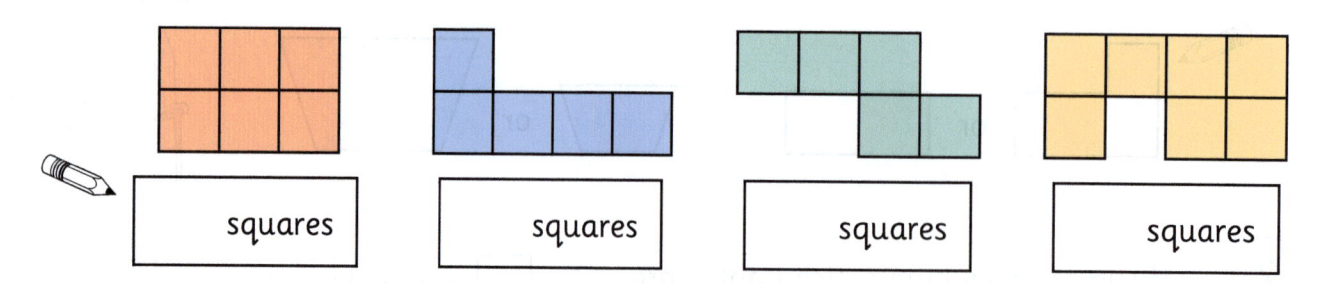

☐ squares   ☐ squares   ☐ squares   ☐ squares

2 Draw lines to match each shape to its area. One has been done for you.

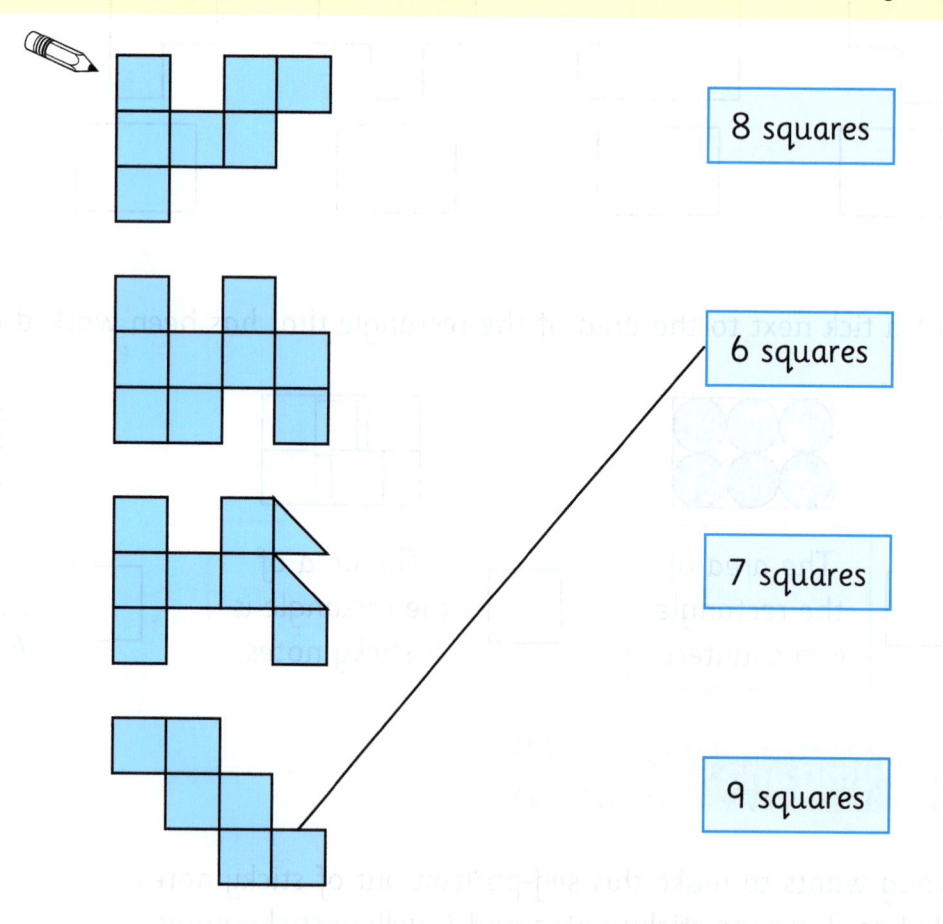

8 squares

6 squares

7 squares

9 squares

3 Use the times table fact to work out the area of this rectangle.

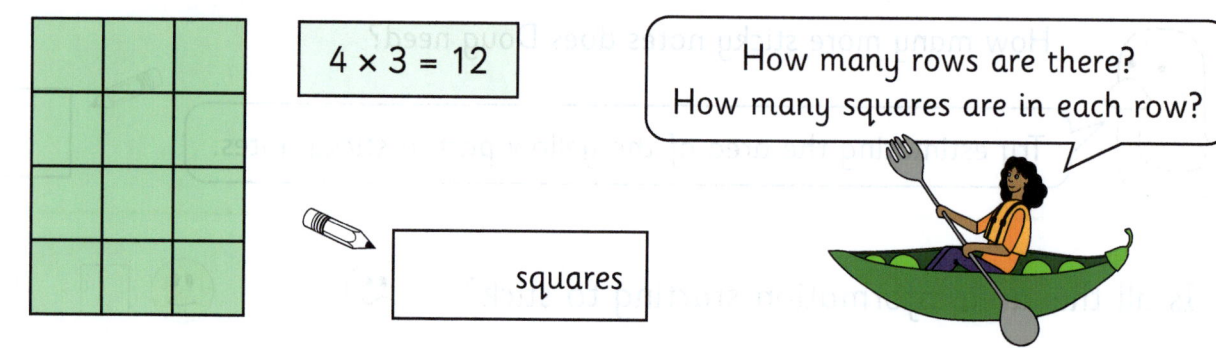

4 × 3 = 12

☐ squares

How many rows are there?
How many squares are in each row?

Block 3 — Area — Step 2

④ Each drawing is made up of shapes.
Colour in the shapes that have an area of 4 squares.

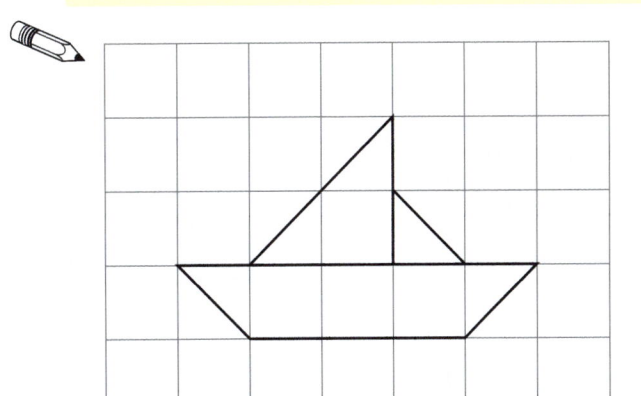

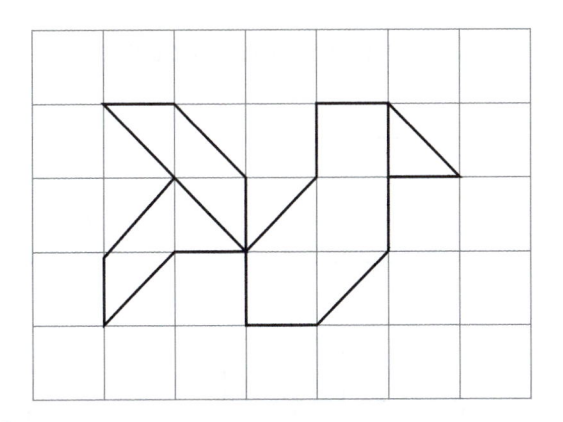

Problem Solving and Reasoning

⑤ Coral made a mistake when working out the area of this arrow. She thinks the area is 10 squares.

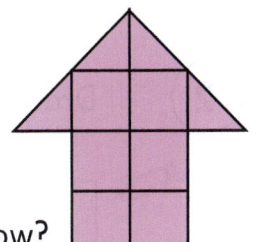

What did Coral do wrong? What is the correct area of the arrow?

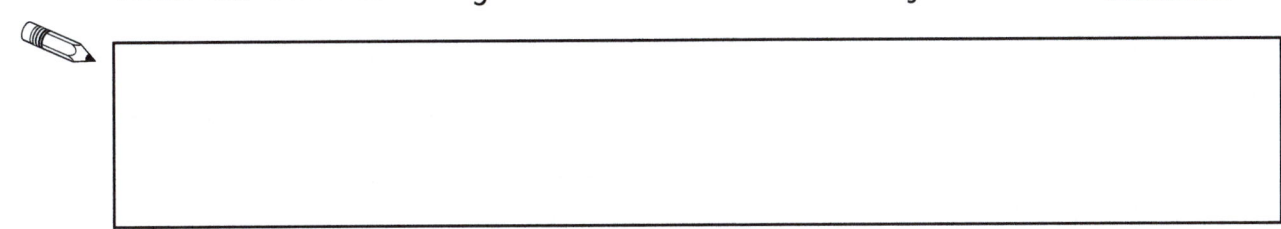

⑥ Roger and Polly are playing a game. Polly has hidden 6 ships in the grid below, following these rules:

1. Each ship must be a rectangle.
2. Ships must not touch any other ships, even diagonally.

Roger has found 5 of the ships so far. The final ship has the largest area. Work out where the final ship is and draw it on the grid.

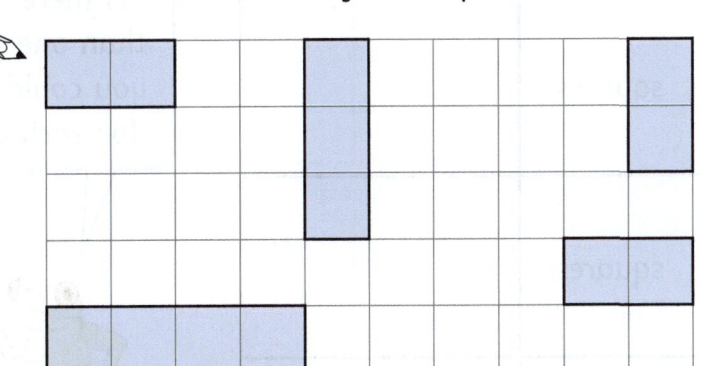

Work out the areas of the other ships. How big does the final ship need to be?

Has counting squares been plain sailing?

Block 3 — Area — Step 2

Making Shapes

1 Circle the shapes that are rectilinear.

2 Draw 3 different rectilinear shapes that have an area of 6 squares.

3 In each row of the table, work out the area of the first rectilinear shape. Then draw another rectilinear shape that has the same area.

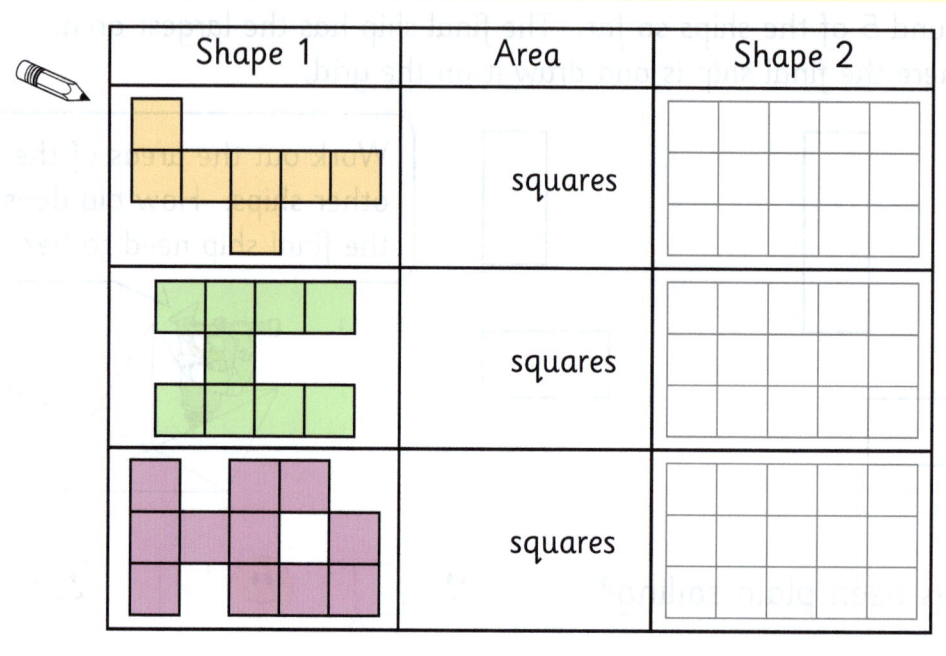

Shape 1	Area	Shape 2
	squares	
	squares	
	squares	

Is there more than one shape you could draw for each area?

Block 3 — Area — Step 3

④ Colour in an odd number of squares to make this shape a rectangle.

Can you make this a rectangle by colouring in an even number of squares instead?

⑤ Add more squares to each rectilinear shape to make rectangles with an area of 18 squares. Make two different rectangles.

⑥ Add exactly 11 squares to the grid to make two squares.

What different sized squares could you make by adding squares to the first shape?

Problem Solving and Reasoning

⑦ Tammy has worked out the area of the rectilinear shape she is holding.

The shape is made up of two overlapping rectangles that each have an area of 8 squares. So the area of the shape is 8 + 8 = 16 squares.

Do you agree with Tammy? Explain your answer.

How are your rectilinear skills shaping up?

Block 3 — Area — Step 3

Comparing Area

1 Compare the area of each pair of shapes then fill in the box with <, > or =.

2 Write numbers in the boxes to put these shapes in order from smallest area (1) to largest area (5).

3 Look at the shapes then complete the sentences.

The shape with the smallest area is Shape ☐.

Shape ☐ has a larger area than Shape Y.

Shape Z has the same area as Shape ☐.

Problem Solving and Reasoning

4 Doug lives in one of the lakes shown on the right. Using the statements about Doug's lake, work out which it could be.

- Doug's lake has the same area as another lake.
- Doug's lake has a bigger area than Lake D.

Doug's lake could be Lake ☐ or Lake ☐.

How did you get along with this page?

Block 3 — Area — Step 4

Block 4 — Multiplication and Division A

Multiples of 3

1 Starting at 15, count forwards to 30 in steps of 3.

15 , ☐ , ☐ , ☐ , ☐ , ☐

2 Work out:

How far can you count up in multiples of 3?

5 lots of 3 = ☐   8 lots of 3 = ☐   6 lots of 3 = ☐

3 Draw lines to match each calculation to its answer.

| 12 × 3 | 7 × 3 | 9 × 3 | 5 × 3 | 11 × 3 |

| 21 | 36 | 15 | 33 | 27 |

Problem Solving and Reasoning

4 Birds have laid eggs in the trees below.
Use the information to find the total number of eggs.

The **oak** has three times as many eggs as the birch.

The **birch** has three times as many eggs as the willow.

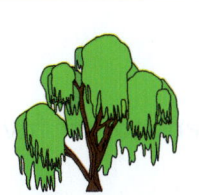

The **willow** has four eggs.

☐ eggs

How did you do on a scale of 1 to 3?

Block 4 — Multiplication and Division A — Step 1

Multiplying and Dividing by 6

1) Some musical notes come in groups of four.

How many groups of notes are there?

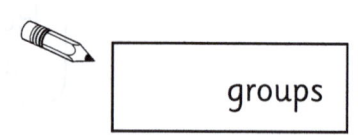

☐ groups

How many notes are there in total?

☐ notes

Can you use your answers to find some multiplication and division facts?

2) Fill in the bar models and complete the matching sentences.

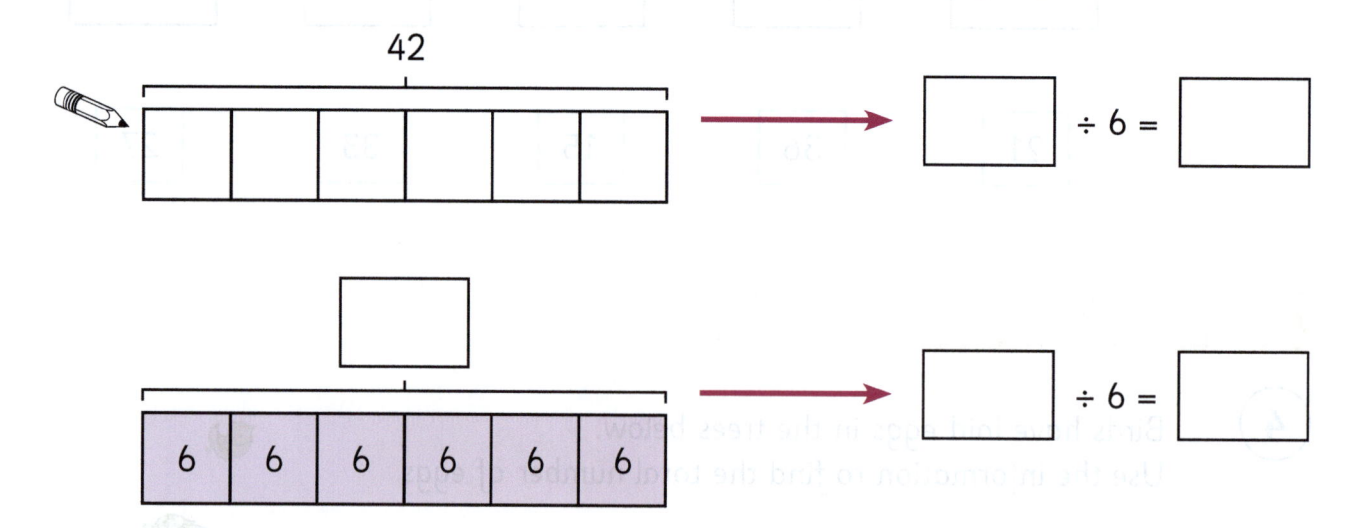

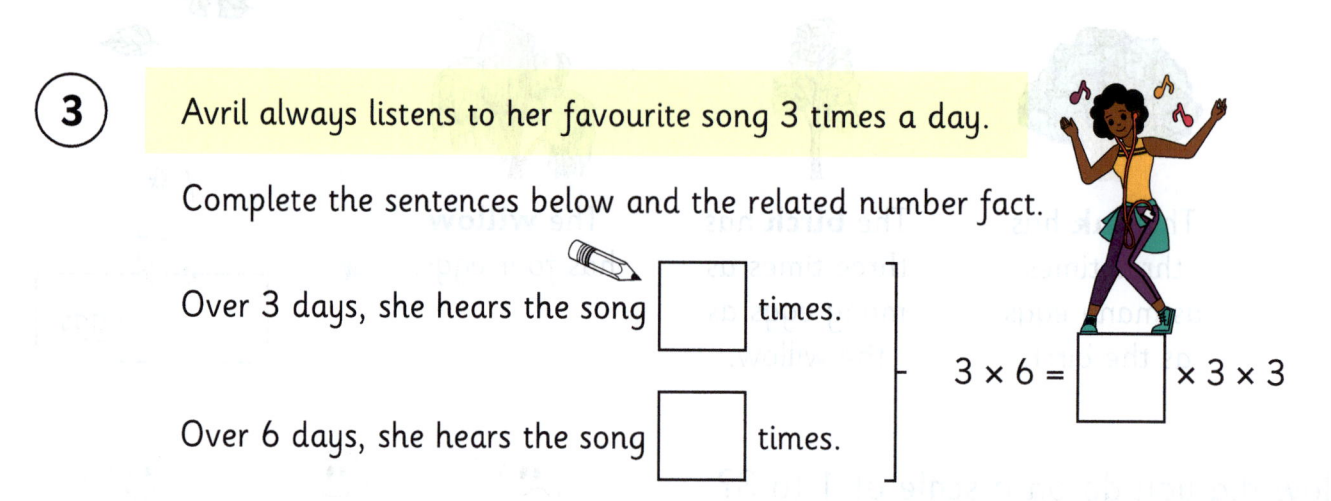

42

☐ ÷ 6 = ☐

| 6 | 6 | 6 | 6 | 6 | 6 |

☐ ÷ 6 = ☐

3) Avril always listens to her favourite song 3 times a day.

Complete the sentences below and the related number fact.

Over 3 days, she hears the song ☐ times.

Over 6 days, she hears the song ☐ times.

3 × 6 = ☐ × 3 × 3

Block 4 — Multiplication and Division A — Step 2

4 Complete the sentences.

9 lots of 6 is ▢   66 shared into 6 equal groups is ▢

5 lots of 6 is ▢   48 shared into 6 equal groups is ▢

3 lots of 6 is ▢   24 shared into 6 equal groups is ▢

Problem Solving and Reasoning

5 A guitar has 6 strings. Simon buys 30 strings to replace all the strings on his guitars. How many guitars does he have?

▢ guitars

6 Ali and Tom count two different rhythms. Ali counts eight lots of three equal beats in 30 seconds. Tom counts eight lots of six equal beats in 30 seconds.

Complete the sentences below.

Ali counts ▢ beats in total.

Tom counts ▢ beats in total.

In the time it takes Ali to count 15 beats, Tom counts ▢ beats.

Do you need to practise multiple times?

Block 4 — Multiplication and Division A — Step 2

6 Times Table Facts

1 Write two multiplication and two division facts to match the groups.

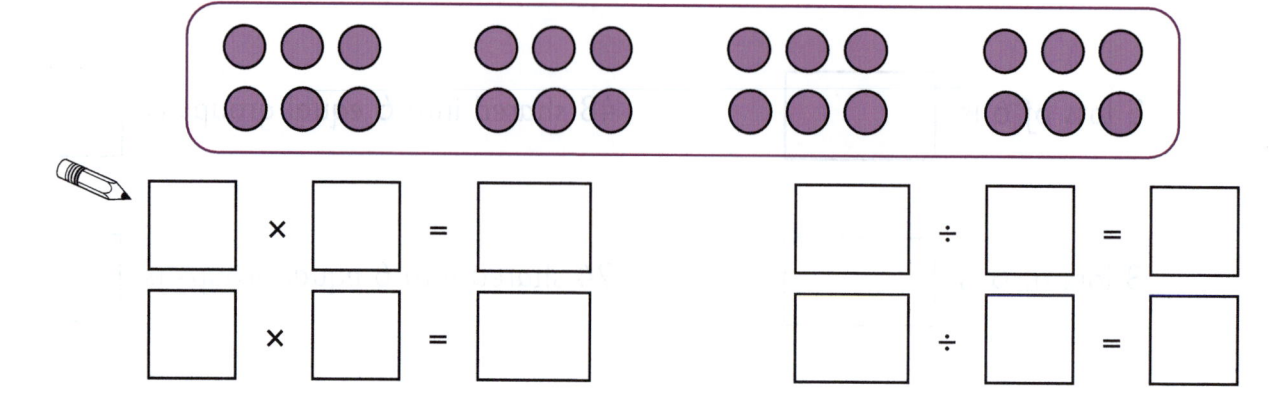

☐ × ☐ = ☐   ☐ ÷ ☐ = ☐

☐ × ☐ = ☐   ☐ ÷ ☐ = ☐

2 Fill in the diagrams.

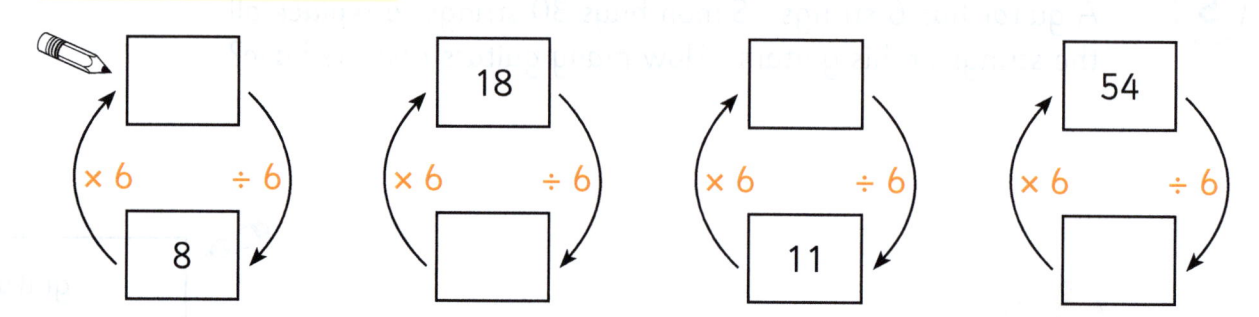

☐ ×6 / ÷6 → 8

18 ×6 / ÷6 → ☐

☐ ×6 / ÷6 → 11

54 ×6 / ÷6 → ☐

3 Complete the number sentences below.

12 × 5 = ☐   and   12 × 1 = ☐ ⟶ 12 × 6 = ☐ + ☐

Problem Solving and Reasoning

4 Write down the 2-digit number that Sam is thinking of.

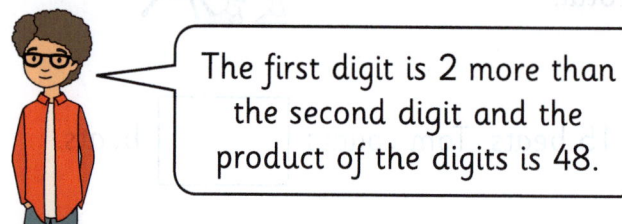

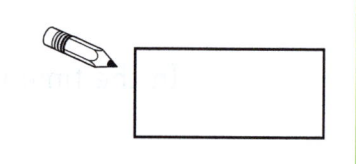

"The first digit is 2 more than the second digit and the product of the digits is 48."

☐

How was this page?

Block 4 — Multiplication and Division A — Step 3

Multiplying and Dividing by 9

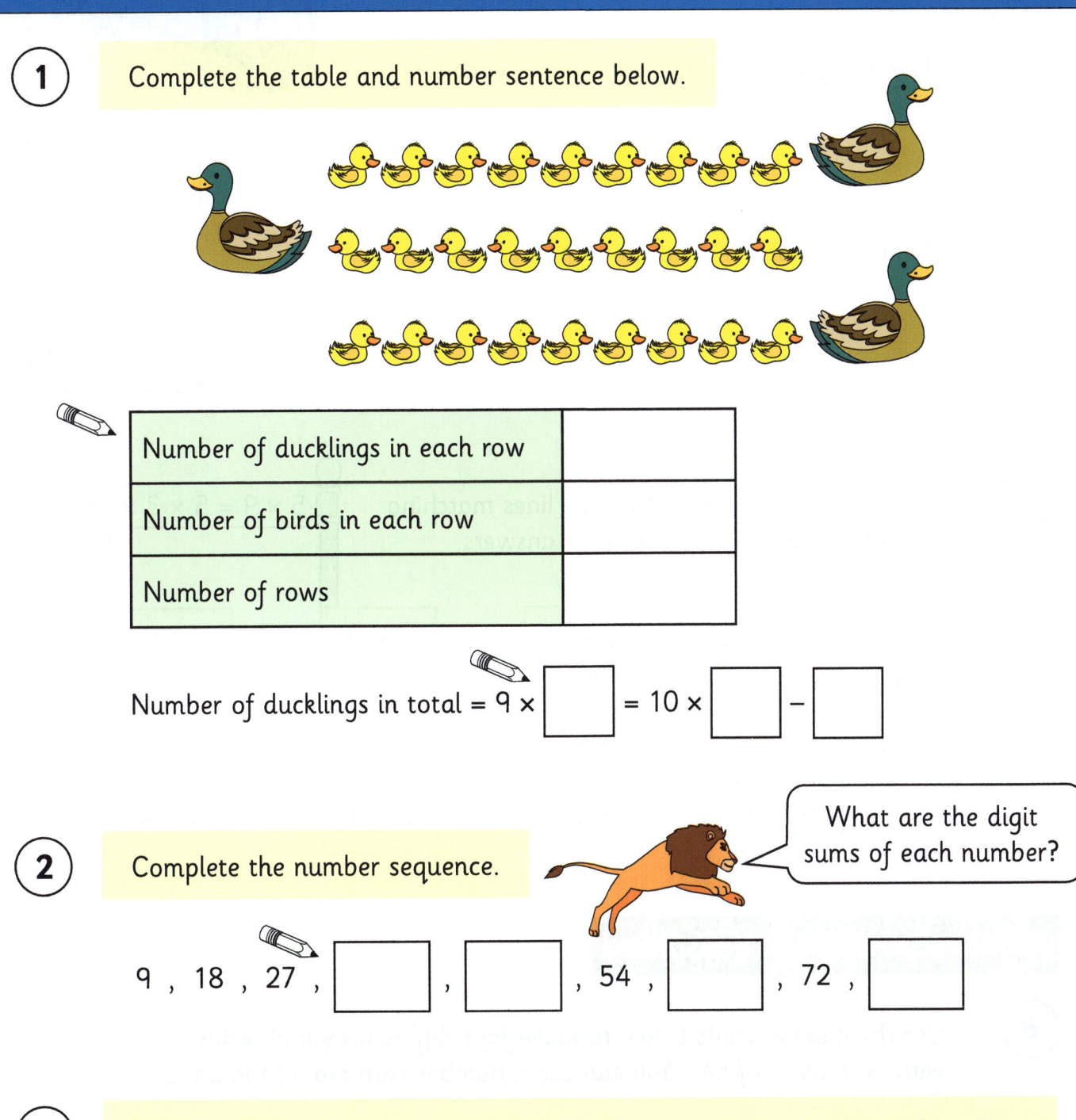

1 Complete the table and number sentence below.

Number of ducklings in each row	
Number of birds in each row	
Number of rows	

Number of ducklings in total = 9 × ☐ = 10 × ☐ − ☐

2 Complete the number sequence.

What are the digit sums of each number?

9 , 18 , 27 , ☐ , ☐ , 54 , ☐ , 72 , ☐

3 Adham always puts 9 books on each shelf of his bookcase. He has 5 shelves.

How many books are there in total?

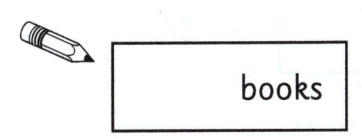

☐ books

How many more shelves will Adham need if he buys 36 more books?

☐ shelves

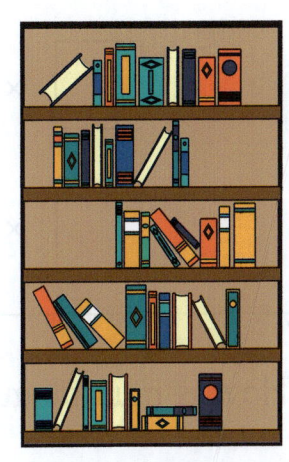

Block 4 — Multiplication and Division A — Step 4

4 108 sacks of flour are divided equally between 9 lorries. Each sack has a mass of 9 kg.

How many sacks of flour are there in each lorry?

☐ sacks

What is the total mass of flour in one lorry?

☐ kg

5 Use the clue on the right to draw lines matching the multiplications with the same answers.

5 × 9 = 5 × 3 × 3

1 × 9   4 × 9   2 × 9   8 × 9

24 × 3   3 × 3   6 × 3   12 × 3

Problem Solving and Reasoning

6 Use the number cards below to make four different multiplications with an answer of 54. You can use a number card more than once.

3   9   6

☐ × ☐ = 54   ☐ × ☐ = 54

☐ × ☐ × ☐ = 54   ☐ × ☐ × ☐ = 54

How is multiplying and dividing by 9?

Block 4 — Multiplication and Division A — Step 4

9 Times Table Facts

1 Put the numbers into their correct positions in the table.

27   79   53   81   19   18

Multiple of 9	Not a multiple of 9

2 Work out the calculations.

5 × 9 = ☐   7 × 9 = ☐   12 × 9 = ☐

9 ÷ 9 = ☐   54 ÷ 9 = ☐   36 ÷ 9 = ☐

3 Fill in the gaps in the sentences.

6 × 10 = ☐ and 6 × 1 = ☐ , so 6 × 9 = ☐

12 × 9 = ☐ and 1 × 9 = ☐ , so 13 × 9 = ☐

Problem Solving and Reasoning

4 Tanya has noticed something about multiples of 9.

"The digit sums of multiples of 9 are also multiples of 9."

Use this information to circle the multiples of 9 below.

837   209   773

119   999   459

Did this page have you dancing with joy?

Block 4 — Multiplication and Division A — Step 5

3, 6 and 9 Times Tables

1 Complete the table.

What do you notice about each row and column?

	× 3	× 6	× 9
2			
4			
8			
12			

2 Fill in the bar models.

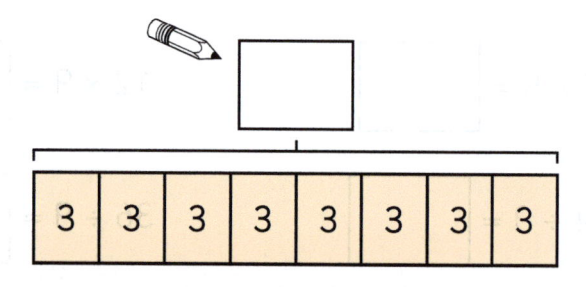

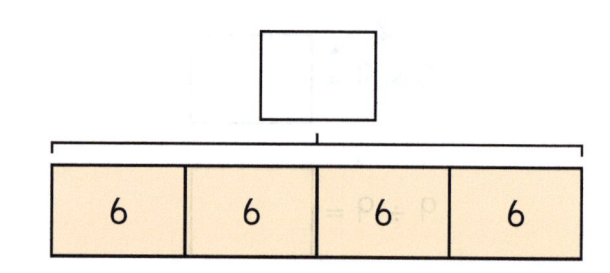

☐
| 3 | 3 | 3 | 3 | 3 | 3 | 3 | 3 |

☐
| 6 | 6 | 6 | 6 |

Problem Solving and Reasoning

3 5 groups of 3 dancers perform with 6 groups of 5 dancers.

Can all the dancers perform in groups of nine?
Explain your answer.

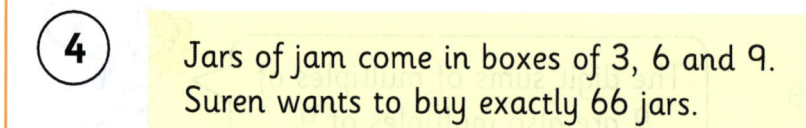

4 Jars of jam come in boxes of 3, 6 and 9.
Suren wants to buy exactly 66 jars.

What is the smallest number of boxes he can buy?
Explain your answer.

How confident are you with all these tables?

Block 4 — Multiplication and Division A — Step 6

Multiplying and Dividing by 7

1) Each of these ships has five sails.

How many ships are there?

☐ ships

How many sails are there in total?

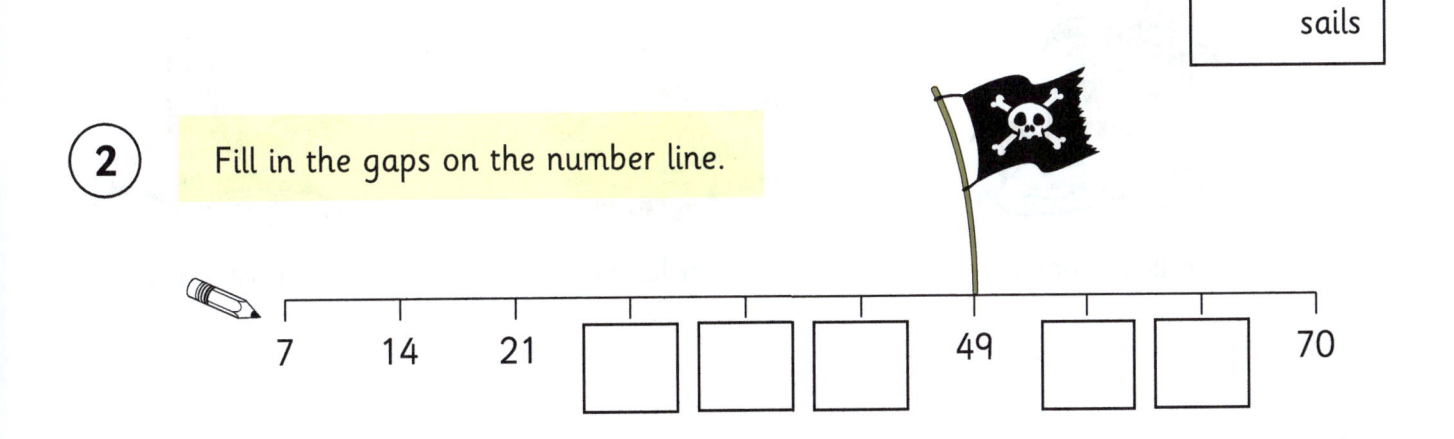

☐ sails

2) Fill in the gaps on the number line.

7, 14, 21, ☐, ☐, ☐, 49, ☐, ☐, 70

3) Use the arrays of anchors to help you complete the number sentences.

$2 \times 7 = 2 \times \boxed{} + 2 \times 2$

$5 \times 7 = 3 \times \boxed{} + 2 \times 7$

Block 4 — Multiplication and Division A — Step 7

4 A kraken can sink 3 ships using one tentacle. How many ships can it sink using 7 tentacles?

☐ ships

5 The distance between Yellow Sands and Thunder Rock is seven times the distance between Thunder Rock and Lost Lagoon.

Use the information to complete the diagram.

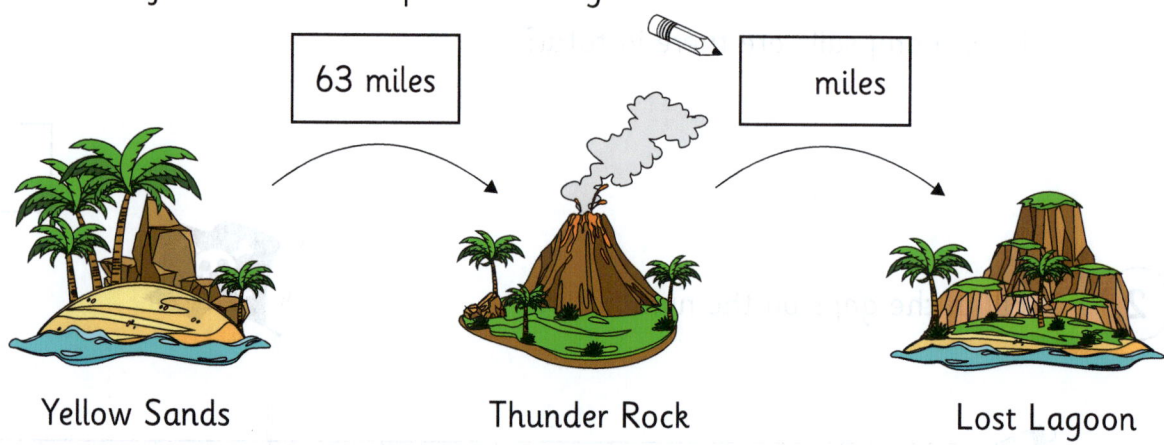

63 miles ☐ miles

Yellow Sands   Thunder Rock   Lost Lagoon

Problem Solving and Reasoning

6 Swashbuckle Steve goes on a voyage and collects the treasure below.

- Rubies and diamonds are each worth seven gold coins.
- Emeralds are worth two gold coins.

What is the total value of the jewels he collects on his voyage?

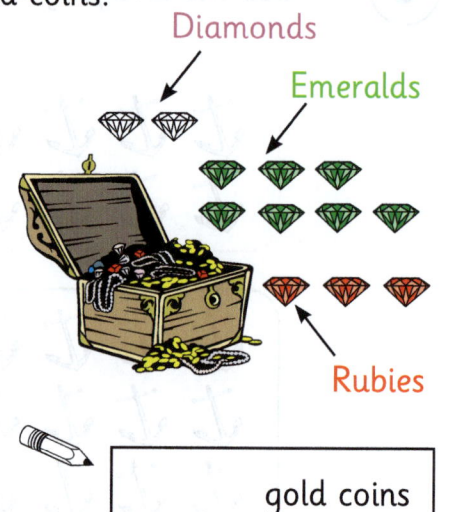

☐ gold coins

Arrr you happy with this topic?

Block 4 — Multiplication and Division A — Step 7

7 Times Table Facts

1 Draw lines to match each calculation to its answer.

| 9 × 7 | 7 × 7 | 77 ÷ 7 | 7 × 6 | 28 ÷ 7 |

| 63 | 11 | 4 | 49 | 42 |

2 Fill in the gaps to complete the 7 times table facts.

8 × 7 = ☐ × 3 + ☐ × 5   8 × 7 = 8 × 9 − 8 × ☐

3 Write an inverse operation for each calculation.

9 × 7 = 63 → ☐ ÷ ☐ = ☐

11 × 7 = 77 → ☐ ÷ ☐ = ☐

Problem Solving and Reasoning

4 Use the clues to find the 2-digit number.

- The number is between 5 × 7 and 7 × 7
- The first digit is greater than 21 ÷ 7
- The second digit is equal to 56 ÷ 7

The number is: ☐

How do you find the seven times table?

11 Times Table Facts

1) Write down the numbers shown by each group of place value counters, then complete the calculations.

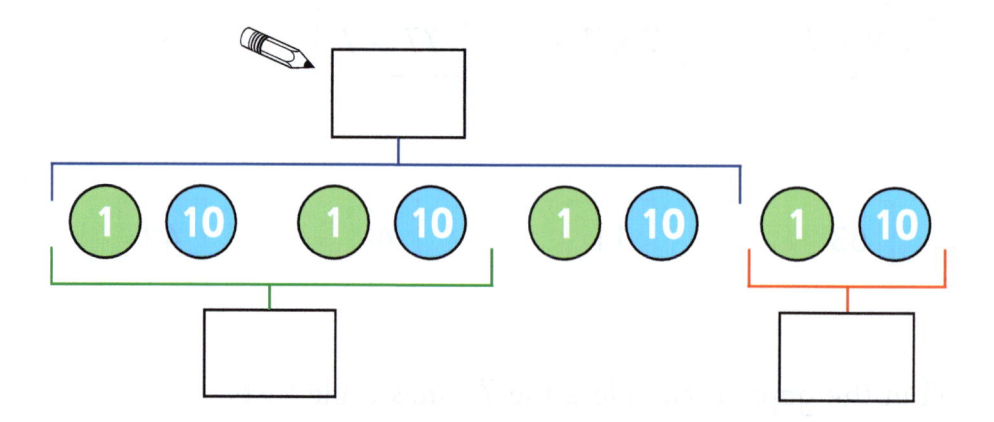

11 × 2 = ☐   11 × 3 = ☐   11 × 4 = ☐

2) Fill in the gaps in the bar models.

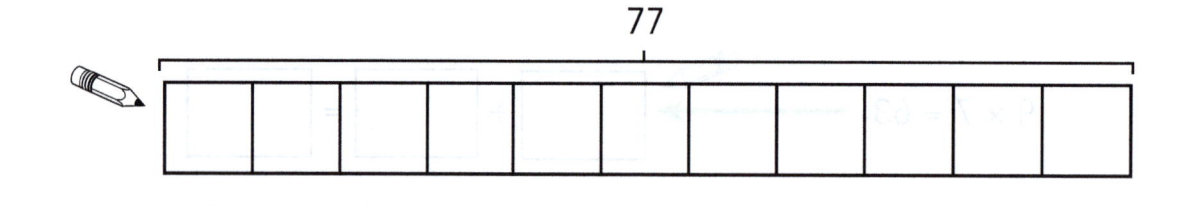

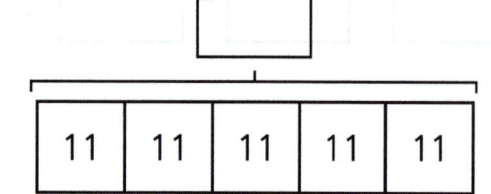

77

Why isn't 11 × 12 equal to 1212?

3) Complete the calculations represented by the base 10 blocks below.

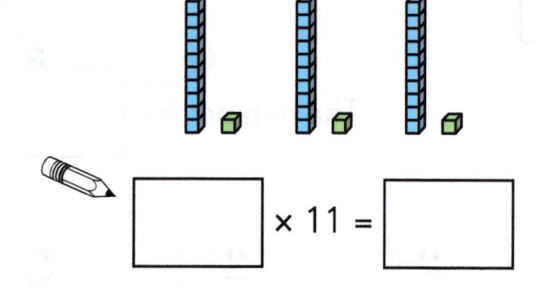

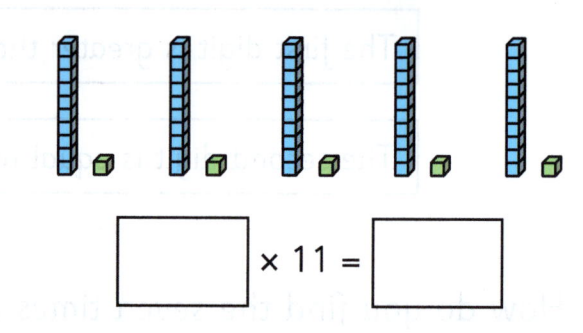

☐ × 11 = ☐   ☐ × 11 = ☐

Block 4 — Multiplication and Division A — Step 9

4 Complete the diagrams below.

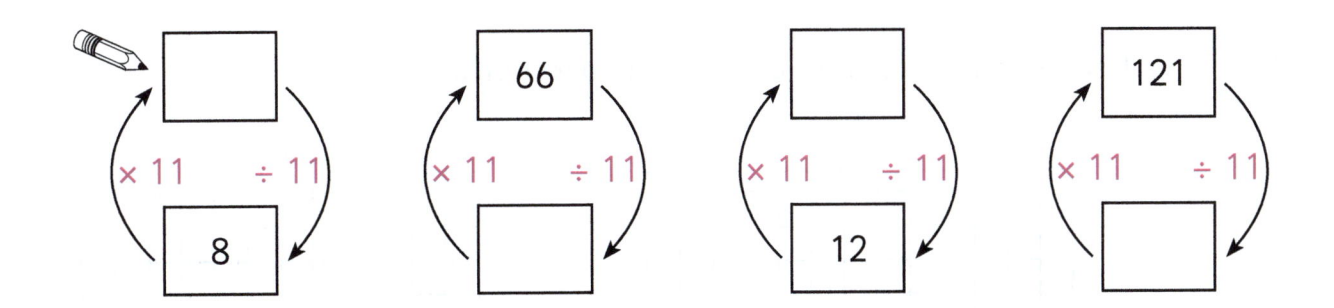

Diagram 1: top box empty, bottom box 8, ×11 / ÷11
Diagram 2: top box 66, bottom box empty, ×11 / ÷11
Diagram 3: top box empty, bottom box 12, ×11 / ÷11
Diagram 4: top box 121, bottom box empty, ×11 / ÷11

5 Eleven robots each have two power supplies, four wheels and five sensors.

Complete the table below.

Total number of power supplies	
Total number of wheels	
Total number of sensors	

Problem Solving and Reasoning

6 Model 1 of Maths Bot can complete a calculation in 77 seconds. Each new model of Maths Bot that comes out can complete the calculation 11 seconds faster than the previous model.

Complete the sentences.

Model 2 takes

77 − ☐ = ☐ × 11 = ☐ seconds

Model 3 takes

77 − ☐ = ☐ × 11 = ☐ seconds

Model 5 takes

77 − ☐ = ☐ × 11 = ☐ seconds

Were you speedy with those times tables?

Block 4 — Multiplication and Division A — Step 9

12 Times Table Facts

1 Use the arrays to work out the multiplications.

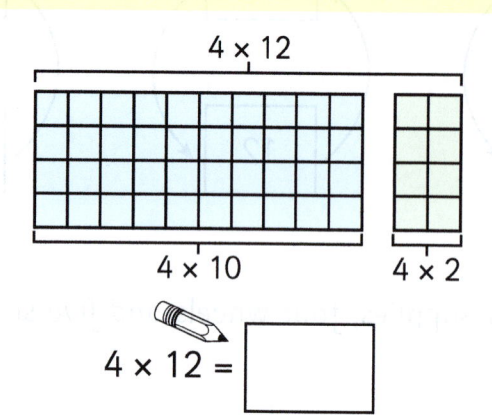

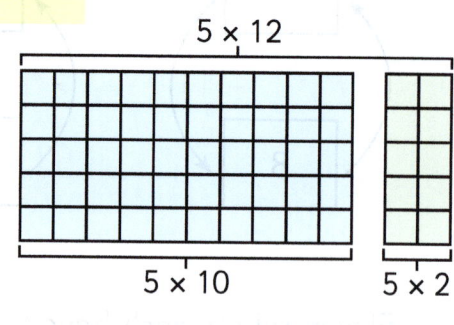

4 × 12
4 × 10   4 × 2

5 × 12
5 × 10   5 × 2

4 × 12 = ☐

5 × 12 = ☐

2 Fill in the blanks on the number line.

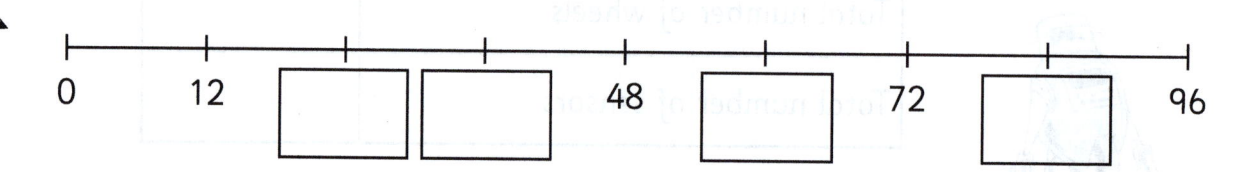

0 — 12 — ☐ — ☐ — 48 — ☐ — 72 — ☐ — 96

3 Eggs come in boxes of 12.

James buys 3 boxes. How many eggs does he get? ☐ eggs

Becki needs 25 eggs for a recipe. She buys 2 boxes. Does she have enough eggs for her recipe? ☐

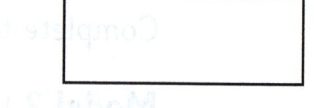

4 Circle all the numbers below that are in the 12 times table.

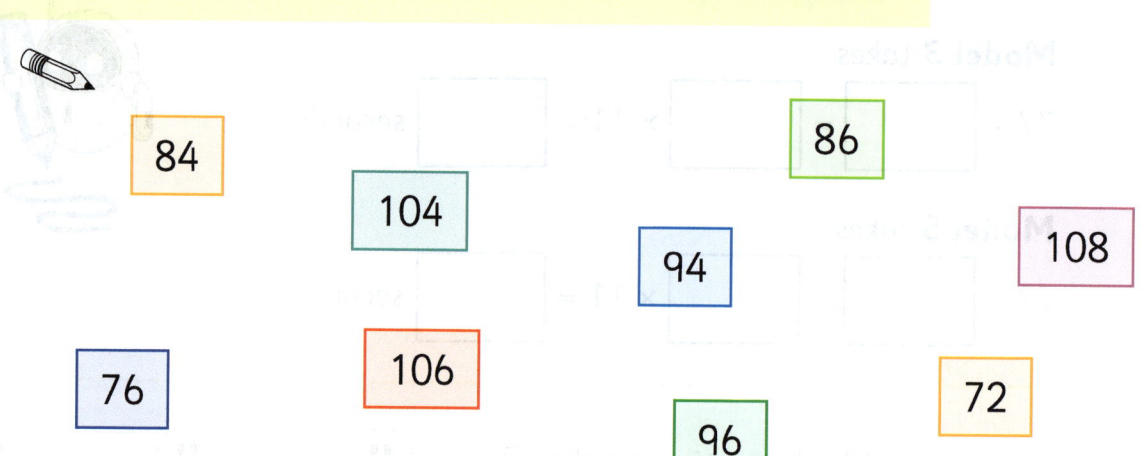

84   104   86   108   76   106   94   96   72

Block 4 — Multiplication and Division A — Step 10

5) Fill in the blanks in these sentences.

6 lots of 12 is ☐.   ☐ times 12 is 96.

☐ lots of 12 is 132.   12 times 12 is ☐.

Problem Solving and Reasoning

6) Marianne uses this method to multiply harder numbers by 12.

$23 \times 12 = 23 \times 10 + 23 \times 2$
$= 230 + 46$
$= 276$

Do you think my method is useful? How else could you work this out?

Use Marianne's method to work out 15×12.

7) Some students have made some claims about the 12 times table. For each, say if they are always true, sometimes true, or never true.

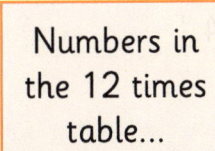

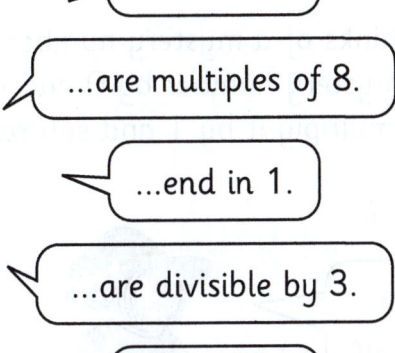

Numbers in the 12 times table...

...are even.

...are multiples of 8.

...end in 1.

...are divisible by 3.

...end in 2.

'Dozen' that topic seem alright now?

Block 4 — Multiplication and Division A — Step 10

Multiplying a Number by 1 and 0

1 Use the options in the box to complete the sentences.

Any number multiplied by 1 is ☐.

Any number multiplied by 0 is ☐.

| 0 | 1 | itself |
| doubled | halved |

2 Fill in the missing numbers in these calculations.

5 × 1 = ☐   7 × 0 = ☐   6 × ☐ = 0

8 × ☐ = 8   11 × ☐ = 0   12 × 1 = ☐

3 Kari is making 9 goodie bags for her birthday party. Each bag needs to contain 1 lollipop, and 0 gold bars.

How many of each item does she need?

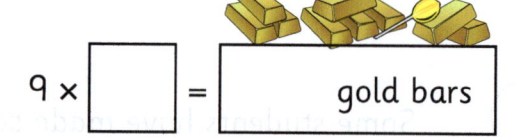

9 × ☐ = ☐ lollipops   9 × ☐ = ☐ gold bars

Problem Solving and Reasoning

4 The Magical Miss Melville thinks of a mystery number. She says, "If I multiply my mystery number by 0 and add 5, I get the same result as if I multiply it by 1 and subtract 4."

What is her mystery number?

Can you think of your own mystery number and give your partner clues to work it out?

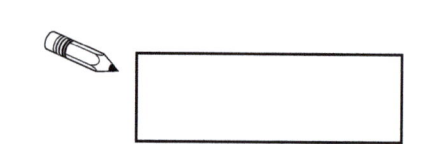

Can you multiply by 1 and 0?

Block 4 — Multiplication and Division A — Step 11

Dividing a Number by 1 and Itself

1 Use the cactus plants to fill in the blanks.

6 can be shared into:

☐ equal group(s) of 1   or   ☐ equal group(s) of 6

6 ÷ 1 = ☐   6 ÷ 6 = ☐

2 Work out these divisions.

3 ÷ 1 = ☐   2 ÷ 2 = ☐   8 ÷ 1 = ☐   11 ÷ 11 = ☐

3 Circle all the calculations that give an answer of 1.

7 ÷ 1   12 ÷ 12   4 ÷ 4   5 ÷ 10

9 ÷ 9   2 ÷ 1   11 ÷ 10   1 ÷ 1   5 ÷ 5

Problem Solving and Reasoning

4 The Magical Miss Melville is back with another mystery number. She says, "If I divide my mystery number by itself, I get 1 less than what I get if I divide it by 1."

What is her mystery number this time?

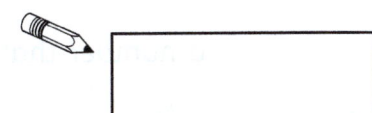

☐

Have you mastered this topic?

Block 4 — Multiplication and Division A — Step 12

Multiplying 3 Numbers

1 Fill in the boxes to show two methods for working out 11 × 3 × 2.

11 × 3 × 2 = ☐ × 2 = ☐

11 × 3 × 2 = 11 × ☐ = ☐

Which way round do you think is easier? Why?

2 Work out these multiplications.

5 × 2 × 5 = ☐ × ☐ = ☐

4 × 3 × 3 = ☐ × ☐ = ☐

7 × 1 × 9 = ☐ × ☐ = ☐

6 × 2 × 4 = ☐ × ☐ = ☐

Problem Solving and Reasoning

3 Look at these number cards.   [2] [5] [8] [3] [12]

Pick three cards that multiply together to give...

...a number that ends in 0: ☐ × ☐ × ☐ = ☐

...a 3-digit number: ☐ × ☐ × ☐ = ☐

...a number that starts with 7: ☐ × ☐ × ☐ = ☐

How did you find this page?

Block 4 — Multiplication and Division A — Step 13